In the Field

In the Field

Readings on the Field Research Experience

**Edited by Carolyn D. Smith
and William Kornblum**

PRAEGER

New York
Westport, Connecticut
London

GN
346
.I5
1989

Library of Congress Cataloging-in-Publication Data

In the field: readings on the field research experience / edited by
  Carolyn D. Smith and William Kornblum.
      p. cm.
    Bibliography: p.
    Includes index.
    ISBN 0–275–93317–2 (alk. paper). — ISBN 0–275–93319–9 (pbk. :
  alk. paper)
    1. Ethnology—Field work. 2. Participant observation. 3. Social
  sciences—Field work. I. Smith, Carolyn D. II. Kornblum, William.
  GN346.I5 1989
  306'.072—dc20   89–33961

Library of Congress Catalog Card Number: 89–33961
ISBN: 0–275–93317–2

First published in 1989

Praeger Publishers, One Madison Avenue, New York, NY 10010
A division of Greenwood Press, Inc.

Printed in the United States of America

The paper used in this book complies with the Permanent
Paper Standard issued by the National Information Standards
Organization (Z39.48-1984).

10 9 8 7 6 5 4 3 2 1

Contents

Preface

Social scientists who engage in ethnographic field research often become deeply involved in the lives of the people they are studying. In some cases the researcher actually becomes a member of the group or community and participates fully in its day-to-day activities. This experience can have a profound effect on the researcher, who often must reexamine his or her values and attitudes and may be forced to make choices that would not be required in the ordinary course of events. This collection of readings from ethnographic researchers' personal accounts is intended to give students and other readers a taste of what it is really like to conduct research "in the field."

The selections in this book do not focus on methodology, although all of the contributors to this volume are known for their ethnographic research skills. Moreover, while they all believe in the value of this research method, they understand its limitations and recognize that it could not exist independently of other approaches. Yet to varying degrees their experiences in the field have shaped their subsequent research endeavors and, often, their outlook on life.

This volume presents a set of personal accounts by practicing field researchers. It is about how they do their research and how they feel while they are doing it. The authors describe how they became accepted by the people they wished to know, how they built and maintained relationships with their subjects, how they worked to maintain their objectivity as researchers, and how they sorted through their research findings and worried about the privacy of the friends they had made in the field.

The editors would like to take this opportunity to thank all of the contributors to this volume for their generous support and cooperation.

In the Field

William Kornblum

Introduction

When night fell the family gathered around the campfire, and when the early part of the evening passed without incident, the young adults drifted beyond the limits of the fire. The older Boyash [gypsies] continued to trade stories over the remaining wine and coffee. Then, just as they were dispersing, a small hail of stones landed around the main courtyard of the camp.

Within seconds the family was readying itself for bloody battle. Most of those who had lingered around the fire were women and, incensed at the resumption of hostilities, they ran from wagon to wagon summoning the men and gathering all available weapons. I had retired to my *roulotte* [wagon] and was about to undress for bed when Persa burst into the wagon. She shouted that the Serbians were throwing stones again; we were going out to stop them. I would have hesitated, flattered that the family felt so comfortable with me that they would ask me to fight on their behalf. I was also worried about getting hurt. But Persa had no sympathy for the distinction between participant and observer. She thrust a heavy stick in my hand and shoved me toward the door.

As I found my way to the main road through the camp, my worst fears were confirmed. It seemed there would be a pitched battle, for the Boyash men and women were grouped about 50 yards away from a much larger group of Serbian men. Both groups were heavily armed. I saw Cortez flick open his switchblade. Tony was holding a shotgun. The Boyash women kept up a steady barrage of violent oaths and insults. As we slowly advanced toward the Serbians I attempted to find a place in the second ranks, but Persa was there again to shove me to the front.

This is an excerpt from the field notes I wrote during a research sojourn with Boyash gypsies in a shantytown on the outskirts of Paris. It describes a dispute between "my" family of gypsies and a nearby encampment of Serbian immigrants. For the family with whom I was living at the time, the importance of the incident lay in the fact that they had demonstrated their willingness to defend their honor, using violence if necessary. For me, a foreign ethnographer and participant observer, it was significant because despite my ambivalence and fear I had stood with "my" people in the face of danger. In a moment of crisis I had become one of them.

Ethnographic research is not always this exciting or dangerous. The ethnographer's goal is to describe the way of life of a particular group from within, that is, by understanding and communicating not only what happens but how the members of the group interpret and understand what happens. The primary technique used in ethnographic research is participant observation, which usually involves living or otherwise spending extended periods with the people one is trying to understand.

Usually the most trying aspect of this kind of research is the effort to obtain permission to spend time with the people one wishes to get to know. Once this is accomplished (and it is never entirely achieved), the work of observation and description can become, on the surface, quite routine and even boring. One is there day after day, watching and gently asking questions. At times the questions are annoying; one's very presence may become a drag. From the standpoint of those being observed, the observer is ignorant of the most obvious truths and constantly exposes that ignorance by questioning behavior that everyone else takes for granted. In short, our respondents often find us tiresome unless we have something to offer them other than just our goodwill. Thus, it occurred to Persa that my size would be an asset to the gypsies, so she pushed me to the front line.

Persa and I never discussed that incident (which, happily, was resolved without actual violence), but I could tell that it had changed her opinion of me from one of disdain to one of guarded respect. It is rare for the subjects of ethnographic research to go on record about their feelings regarding the research, but the novelist Ken Kesey offered an insightful metaphor in a speech he gave some years ago. Best known for his gripping but fictional account of life in a mental hospital, *One Flew Over the Cuckoo's Nest,* Kesey himself was the subject of a quasi-ethnographic study: He and his circle of hippie friends, known as the Merry Pranksters, were described by Tom Wolfe in *The Electric Kool-Aid Acid*

Test. In the 1960s Wolfe was just beginning his career as an ethnographic journalist, yet he was already renowned for his steadfast uninvolvement in the lives of his subjects, as well as for his cool white linen suits. One day he was sitting with the Merry Pranksters in a room of Kesey's house while Kesey was painting the ceiling. A glob of yellow paint fell on the observer's immaculate white jacket, and although Wolfe wiped off the paint with studied calmness, he was unable to hide his profound annoyance. "That's how it is, Tom," said Kesey. "If you want to get down in it you've got to get some of it on you."

This comment goes to the heart of the participant observer's dilemma: To what extent does one become involved in and participate in the lives of the people one is observing? All social-scientific ethnographers, and many journalists like Tom Wolfe, experience some version of this dilemma. I experienced it in the incident described earlier, and I have encountered it in one form or another in every field research study I have engaged in. Nor does the researcher have much control over how the dilemma of participation versus observation will present itself. For Douglas Harper, the issue was raised immediately as he learned how to survive as a tramp. For Claire Sterk, too, the issue was raised quite soon after she began spending time with prostitutes on the stroll. For William F. Whyte, the dilemma was present as he befriended the Martini family and became accepted in the community, but it manifested itself most strongly later in his study, when he was asked to work in a local election campaign and found that he was expected to break the law by voting more than once for the same candidate.

Of all the methods employed in modern social science, ethnographic field research requires the most intense involvement with one's subjects. The ethnographer's "presentation of self" and the changes he or she experiences are part of the research process itself. These aspects of the method enrich the data gathered in this way by adding personal and emotional depth, but they also lead to endless complications, as many of the selections in this volume will show.

Those of us who practice the techniques of ethnographic research often write about our experiences as participant observers as well as other aspects of the ethnographic craft. However, our accounts of what we actually do in the field and the adventures we encounter there are usually buried in "methodological appendixes" to our published works. Other people, not ourselves, are the subjects of our research; when we speak of our own experiences in the field, we often do so only as an afterthought. Yet quite frequently these understated accounts of personal fieldwork experiences contain episodes or images that become widely known in their own right: Examples include Whyte's famous account of how he came to know "Doc" in *Street Corner Society;* Elliot Liebow's haunting image of seeing the people of *Tally's Corner* through the spaces

of a chain-link fence; and Barbara Myerhoff's moving description, in
Number Our Days, of how she was tested and badgered by the aged
Jews who spent their time in a senior citizens' center in Venice Beach,
California. In these cases, and in many others as well, the writers' de-
scriptions of their own field research experiences are valuable state-
ments about the nature of ethnographic research.

In recent years the writings of ethnographers have come under a great
deal of scrutiny and criticism.[1] One point that has emerged from this
evaluation is that modern ethnographies are less likely to follow a standard format than were earlier works of this type. Current ethnographies
reflect more of the writers' literary and social-scientific sensibilities than
did earlier studies, which followed a well-known analytical outline. The
generality of this trend and its implications are surely worthy of attention. The authors represented in this volume, however, reflect on the
interpersonal qualities of the ethnographic experience itself. By and large,
they are writing about emotional and other issues associated with this
research style, rather than about the equally vexing problems of meaning
and communication.

It is also worth noting that ethnographic field research is a method in
which one person typically gathers and analyzes the data. Reliance on
individual effort is somewhat uncommon in this age of larger-scale and
more bureaucratic research programs, which employ numerous research
assistants and co-principal investigators. However, even when the ethnographer is employed with others in a larger study—as is often the case
with AIDS or drug research of large-scale policy evaluations—it remains
true that the observer often works alone, equipped with little more than
a notebook and a pen (and at times a tape recorder or a camera). This
was certainly true for each of the authors included here. Yet many of
them had the support of larger organizations that encouraged their efforts and helped sustain them. Liebow's work, for example, was part of
a larger program of research on poverty and opportunity in Washington,
D.C., directed by sociologist Hylan Lewis. Sterk's research was funded
and supervised by the U.S. Centers for Disease Control in Atlanta and
by an agency of the New York State Division of Substance Abuse Studies. Her field notes and much of the data she collected were often used
by other researchers for different purposes. This is also true of the research conducted by Terry Williams, Edmundo Morales, and, to a somewhat lesser extent, Ruth Horowitz and me. Our books are about what
we saw and experienced as individuals, but our research was part of a
larger enterprise and might not have been possible otherwise. In sum,
although ethnography is always a solo enterprise, increasingly the researcher needs the support of other professionals.

*   *   *

Whether they are working alone or as part of a larger research team, the relationships that develop between ethnographic researchers and the people they are studying are critical to the success of their research. Certain key aspects of those relationships serve as the basis of the organization of this book. Part I, "Gaining Trust," deals with the confusing and frustrating period every field researcher goes through while trying to gain acceptance by the people under study. Thus, Elijah Anderson writes about the custom of "going for cousins" (using a fictive kinship term to signify close friendship), which resulted in sponsorship for him as he undertook his research among black men in a low-income neighborhood on Chicago's South Side. (A researcher who has a "sponsor" has the support of a well-known, highly credible member of the community under study.) Carol Stack gained the trust of the women in The Flats largely by being helpful and sympathetic—providing daily assistance with the children or the shopping, listening to complaints about the welfare office, and the like. For Terry Williams the problem was more complex. When a researcher is observing illegal activities, the normal difficulties of gaining trust are compounded by the greater risk respondents run in taking the researcher into their confidence. The researcher also has to find a way of not participating in the illegal activity while still gaining the acceptance of those who are participating in it. In his research on cocaine use in illegal after-hours clubs in New York City, Williams faced these problems as well as others. In his essay he stresses the importance of outward symbols like dress in gaining acceptance. He also explains how he managed to observe cocaine users without using the drug himself.

Part II, "Building Relationships," continues with the theme of gaining the confidence of respondents; it shows how ethnographic researchers often develop subtle, complex relationships with some of their informants. Liebow, Horowitz, and Harper all had to work hard to build and maintain relationships with their subjects. These selections also illustrate the impact of differences in race, gender, and class between the researcher and his or her subjects. Liebow, a white Jew among low-income blacks; Horowitz, a white woman among male Chicano gang members; Harper, a representative of the respectable world of jobs and income, traveling with Carl, a tramp—all had to deal with the disparity between their backgrounds and those of their subjects. As Harper put it, "I never really learned to experience the world as a tramp and I knew that unless I moved completely into that life my values would probably remain in the world of relationships and commitments."

Despite such differences, field researchers persist, continually trying to find ways of reciprocating and empathizing with their subjects. But as illustrated in Part III, "Maintaining Objectivity," empathy itself can become a problem. How do ethnographic researchers deal with the need to be objective, to describe life the way they see it without glossing over unfavorable aspects because of their emotional involvement with the people they are studying? The researcher must not let friendships get in the way of her or his critical faculties. Related to this issue is the question of how deeply to become involved in the lives of the people one is studying. Whyte encountered this problem in the case of repeat voting mentioned earlier, as well as in his participation in community sports—on one occasion, he made the game-winning hit in a neighborhood baseball game. Myerhoff had to cope with the fact that her research was equivalent to a search for her own roots as a Jew, causing her to identify strongly with the elderly Jews whose lives she shared. Sterk obviously could not participate in the day-to-day life of the prostitutes and drug users she was observing, but she was greatly affected by the impact of AIDS on these groups; the mounting death rate and accompanying hopelessness almost caused her to abandon her research. In my own case, the issue of objectivity is illustrated by the episode in which I went out of my way to receive a tongue-lashing from a steel company boss in order to see for myself how he treated employees. One does not ordinarily seek out such an experience, but if I had avoided the incident as my fellow workers recommended, I would have been acting according to their values rather than those of an objective researcher.

Part IV, "The Observer's Role," addresses a special problem of the participant observer. Not only must the observer maintain objectivity, she or he must arrive at some conclusion about the morality of observing other people. In this section, therefore, the researchers step back a little and ask some searching questions about observation itself. Edmundo Morales, Laud Humphreys, and Charles Bosk have observed and written about questionable behaviors. Each has wondered about his right to observe those behaviors, and each has attempted to resolve this issue, although it is not one for which there are any easy solutions.

The book ends with an epilogue that is really a beginning. Like most social-scientific researchers, Vernon Boggs has passionate interests that he would like to convert into an ethnographic study. But he faces the problem of how to move from the amateur's interest to the professional's commitment. This issue is illustrated in Carlos Castaneda's description of his search for "the spot" (el sitio)—the place or area where the observer feels comfortable and is accepted and can begin to participate. Boggs's quest for mentors in the world of salsa, or Afro-Hispanic music, is another version of that search.

NOTE

1. See James Clifford and George F. Marcus, eds., *Writing Culture: The Poetics and Politics of Ethnography* (Berkeley: University of California Press, 1986).

Part I

Gaining Trust

People understand what friendship means. Friends can ask any favor of one another, any time of the night, and it shouldn't make any difference. No one would tell you to drop a friend you can trust.

Carol Stack

Elijah Anderson

Jelly's Place

"Jelly's" is a corner bar and liquor store in a poor black neighborhood on the South Side of Chicago. For three years Elijah Anderson observed the men at Jelly's, hanging out with both working and nonworking men who spent time in the bar. At all times of the day and night and throughout the year, Anderson socialized with the people at Jelly's, talking and listening to them and studying the patterns of interaction that occurred among them.

The purpose of Anderson's research was to discover the social order underlying the interactions among the men who frequented Jelly's. Among other things, he found that a man's rank at Jelly's was indicated by the degree of familiarity expressed in his speech and actions. This ranking process resulted in three fairly distinct categories: regulars (men who are steadily employed and have family ties), wineheads (men who are interested in "gettin' some wine" and "havin' some fun"), and hoodlums (men who care about being "tough" and getting "big money").

Since both Anderson and the men he was observing were black, it was somewhat easier for Anderson to gain acceptance than it might have been for a white observer. However, differences in social class constituted a barrier. When one man asked Anderson what he did for a living and was told that he was a student at the University of Chicago, his reaction was both proud and suspicious.

In this selection Anderson describes some of the interactions in which he participated, as well as the process through which he gained acceptance at Jelly's. In particular, it illustrates the importance of his relationship with Herman, one of the regulars. As often happens in field research, Herman sponsored Anderson; in the words of the men at Jelly's, the two "went for cousins."

Jelly's bar and liquor store has two front entrances, one leading to the barroom and the other to the liquor store. Each room has its own distinctive social character. The barroom is a public place; outfitted with bar stools, a marble-topped counter, and mirrors on the wall, it invites almost anyone to come and promises he will not be bothered as long as he minds his own business. In this sense it is a neutral social area. Yet people who gather on this side of Jelly's tend to be cautiously reserved when approaching others, mainly because on this side they just don't know one another. In contrast, the liquor store is more of a place for peers to hang out and outwardly appears to have a more easygoing, spontaneous ambience.

An open doorway separates the two rooms, and some people gravitate from side to side, the regular clientele usually settling in the liquor store. The social space of the barroom is shared by regular customers and visitors. Sometimes these visitors are people who have been seen around Jelly's but have yet to commit themselves to the setting. Sometimes they are total strangers. At times there will be as many as twenty visitors present, compared with eight or nine regular customers. Regular customers are interspersed among the visitors, but though the space is shared, they seldom come to know one another well. The visitors tend to arrive, get their drinks, sit at the bar for a while, then leave. The regular clientele, on the other hand, do their best to ignore the visitors; they treat them as interlopers. And there exists a certain amount of distrust and suspicion between the two groups.

The strange visitors of the barroom side are usually in the process of making their rounds to various drinking places on the South Side. They pass through Jelly's on their way to someplace else and have a relatively small social stake there. Most of them know few of the regular customers, and they usually do not know Jelly at all; those who do know him often know only that he is the owner of the place. Generally speaking, the regular customers see the visitors as outsiders in search of "action"—"on the hustle," as "trying to get over," or as "trying to get into something." Thus they tend to keep them at some distance and try to seek and maintain advantage during encounters. To the regular customers, the visitors, by and large, remain unknown. This makes for a certain amount of apprehension on the part of both groups and works to maintain distrust between them.

Although most of the visitors respect this definition of affairs, a visitor sometimes ventures into the liquor-store area and begins to hang. He is usually not encouraged to linger. When such a person enters, others usually stop talking or at least quiet down until he leaves. Their eyes follow him, reminding him that he is an intruder. Among the regular clientele he is regarded as an outsider, as one of "Jelly's customers," or even as "just a customer." Sensing that the liquor-store area is either beneath him or apart from him, or that it is too dangerous, the visitor usually finishes his business and returns to the barroom or goes on to another joint. Normally the visitors come to the bar, spend some time, then leave, remaining somewhat unknown to Jelly's regular clientele.

My first few weeks at Jelly's were spent on the barroom side among the visitors and others. This side, for the reasons just stated, was the place most accessible to new people, where strangers could congregate. It was also a place where I could be relatively unobtrusive, yet somewhat sociable. It was here that the process of getting to know Jelly's began, where increasingly I gained some license to exist and talk openly with people. Initially this meant getting to know the people and becoming somewhat involved in their relationships with one another; becoming familiar with the common, everyday understandings people shared and took for granted, the social rules and expectations they held for one another.

One of my earliest encounters was with a young man named Clarence, a visitor just passing through Jelly's. He asked me what I did for a living. I told him I was a student at the University of Chicago. He looked very surprised, but suspicious.

"When you get out of there, they got to treat you like a white man," he said. He was smiling gently, and he was sincere. He seemed both suspicious and a bit proud of my being at the university.

"How do you like it?" he asked cautiously.

"I like it all right," I said.

"You quite a ways from there, aren't you," he said in a half-stating, half-questioning way.

"Yeah, but I got a car," I said. "I come over here once in a while to get a drink and relax."

"Yeah, you got to get away from all them honkies after a while. I know how it is," he said. "Where do you stay?"

"Near Fifty-third and Harper," I answered.

"I know that area pretty good—used to hang out over there back in the fifties,'' he said. Clarence then mentioned some joints we both knew. From that point on we had easy conversation, laughing and talking, watching the people come and go.

Clarence offered to buy me a beer. I accepted and we kept talking. The jukebox blared and people continued to enter and leave, shouting, laughing, meeting friends. Rose, the barmaid, seemed to be enjoying her work, as she laughed and talked between serving up drinks.

As I finished each beer, Clarence would call to Rose and order another Schlitz for me and a gin and tonic for himself. I offered to buy some of the rounds, but he would not let me. For more than two hours we lounged around the barroom of Jelly's, watching the people come and go, gravitating from the barroom to the liquor store and back. The people seemed to be thoroughly enjoying themselves.

"You know, Eli, sometimes I regret I didn't finish high school and go to college. See, I didn't get no education. You got a good chance, you gettin' yourself educated and all, you gon' make something out o' yourself. Hell, get all you can, while you can. Don't be like me. Hell, I wish I could be in your place, goin' to school and all. But I tell you something else. You know, too much education is a bad thing. You can mess around and become a cranium. You ain't no cranium, are you? I hear some of them people at that university are really nutty—out there in left field somewhere. I hope you don't turn out like that. Get all you can, while you can, but don't turn into no cranium.''

After a while our conversation drifted and dragged from topic to topic, and later I decided to go home. I thanked him for the drinks and told him that when I saw him again I would treat him. He told me not to worry about it; that he had really enjoyed talking. We parted and he went his way and I went mine.

The talk between Clarence and me, and the long and involved talks I had with so many other visitors, was more likely to have happened on the barroom side than in the liquor store. It is easier here in part because most of the visitors don't see one another again as buddies and thus may not have an immediate interest in status competition. In a social and emotional sense, their passing relationships can be very open to certain kinds of personal information.

During my first weeks on the barroom side, I became involved in many such conversations. Usually I never saw the person again or, if I did, the relationship would not pick up where it had left off. Seeming somewhat atomized on this side, most people did not seem to expect more than an agreeable and open ear from their counterparts. The visitors I had encountered on occasion came around once in a while, but when they did show up they were often somewhat detached and aloof from the center of things at Jelly's.

After I had been in the field at Jelly's for about four weeks I met

Herman, a 45-year-old janitor. He wore a baggy army fatigue jacket, blue gabardine slacks, and black "keen-toed" shoes. On his head was a beige "high-boy" hat with a black band. Herman was a small brown-skinned man, about five feet eight inches tall and weighing about 145 pounds. At our first meeting I had been sitting at the bar for about twenty minutes, carrying on a conversation with Rose. Herman took the seat next to me and joined in the conversation. In this first encounter, Herman and I talked in much the same way as I had talked with other visitors to the barroom. At this point in the study, of course, I had not yet begun to make careful distinctions among the different types of people at Jelly's; the very notion of visitor, for instance, came to me only later. Herman was witty and seemed very easygoing, yet at times he spoke in a slow drawl. He impressed me as a person experienced on the ghetto streets, for his conversation was spiced with well-placed references to such experiences. Because of my previous encounters in the barroom, which on the whole had not been outstandingly productive, I at first took Herman as just another person I probably would not see again. But, as I was to find out, Herman was not just another visitor, but a member of the regular clientele of Jelly's.

In the course of our initial encounter Herman and I talked briefly but became very involved. Among other things, he mentioned that he had seen me around before, though I had not noticed him. During this conversation, his questions centered on the issue of what I was doing there. Although he never stated this directly, he did ask some leading questions. Not broaching it at first, he led up to it in a subtle conversation of gestures and words. Interested in "who I was," Herman asked me, "What do you do, Eli?" He wanted to know how I spent my time and whether I was gainfully employed. As I was to discover, around Jelly's whether someone works for a living is an important clue to his definition. For most people this helps to determine whether he is to be trusted within the setting, and to what degree.

In response to Herman's inquiries about my occupation, I said, "I'm a graduate student over at the University of Chicago."

"That's nice," said Herman, seeming a little surprised. "How long you been over there?" As I answered his question, he seemed to take this as a kind of license to ask more and more about me. And I took his inquiries as cues that I could do the same. Taking this license, I asked him more about himself. During this exchange of information I noticed a marked change in Herman's demeanor toward me. He became more relaxed and sure of me. He gestured more as he spoke, punctuating his words with hits and jabs to my shoulder. He was a very friendly and affable man. At times I reciprocated by punctuating my own words with smiles and friendly exclamations. On the ghetto streets and in ghetto bars friendly students are not to be feared and suspected but are generally expected to be "square" and bookish. With all the information he had about me, including my willingness to give it, he could place me as "safe" within his own scheme of standards and values.

My openness encouraged Herman to be open with me. As a result, there was now some basis for trust in our relationship. In telling me more about himself, Herman said he was a janitor but quickly added, "I'm a man among men," implying that, contrary to what some might expect of a janitor, he held himself in high esteem. Then he told me about his work and about how early he had to get up in the morning. After more of this familiarizing talk, we parted company on good terms. We had spent more than two hours laughing and talking together. I had held this kind of information exchange with others before, and I didn't expect anything unusual to come from this particular meeting. But it was encounters like this that made me conscious that who I was and how I fit into the cognitive picture of Jelly's did preoccupy some of its more persistent members. When I went to Jelly's the next day, I met Herman again. As I entered the barroom I greeted Rose and others as I usually did. I took a seat at the bar and from my stool watched the activities of the men in the liquor-store room.

In that room people were engaged in spontaneous fun—laughing, yelling, playing with one another, and being generally at ease. To me that room seemed very exciting, but it was clear that I would have been out of place there for it seemed to be only for peer-group members. I sensed that there I would have been reminded of my outsider status again and again. While in the barroom, among the visitors and a few of the peer-group members who gravitated over now and then, I felt *in place*. Looking into the liquor-store room, I saw Herman. Catching his attention, I beckoned to him, and he came over to me in the barroom. We shook hands and greeted each other, then held a friendly conversation over a couple of beers. But soon he returned to the liquor-store area, where more of his buddies seemed to be. That Herman had buddies, and so many of them, was one of the important distinctions between him and many of the visitors I had previously met at Jelly's.

In contrast to the visitors on the barroom side of Jelly's, the regular customers on the liquor-store side tend to be spontaneous, loud, and relatively sure of themselves during interactions. Herman and the others acted very much at home there—and they were. Herman was a very sociable person and seemed to be in and out of everyone's affairs. I could see that very little went on at Jelly's without his knowledge. Recognizing this turned out to have important consequences for my entree to the social world of Jelly's, for it was clear that not many new people stayed around without his soon getting to know them. It became apparent that Jelly's was very much Herman's place; it was his turf, a place where he felt protected from the wrong kind of outsiders.

Apparently he saw me as the right kind of outsider, because when I saw him again in a few days, Herman invited me to share his turf. Again, I was sitting in the barroom, while Herman was laughing and talking with a group of men in the liquor-store room. When I saw them through the open doorway that divided the two areas, I was about to leave. I decided to go through the liquor store to greet Herman, but also to get a closer view of the activity of that room.

As I approached the men I heard Herman say, "Hey, here come my friend, Eli!" Then he said to Sleepy, one of the other men, "He al'right. Hey, this the stud I been tellin' you about. This cat gettin' his doctor's degree." At this point Herman shook my hand and greeted me. I returned the greeting. The others of the group seemed cautious and somewhat incredulous about accepting the "me" presented by Herman. Yet they were polite and approving and remained silent while he and I went through the greeting action. The men just watched, checking us out and talking among themselves. Shortly, Herman began introducing me to the others.

"Hey, Eli. Meet Jake, T. J., and this here's Sleepy." The men then acknowledged me, nodding and saying their hellos. I exchanged greetings with them.

Herman, beer in hand, boasted to the men about a Christmas party he was going to attend where he worked. To make it especially meaningful he accentuated the occasion, describing it as something extravagant and special. He talked of the "foxy chicks" he would be kissing under the mistletoe and of the "intelligent folks" he would be "conversin' " with. Jake responded by saying, "Aw, that nigger's crazy." Other responses were similar, but Herman persisted.

At one point in his presentation Herman invited me to the Christmas party.

"Hey, Eli. You wanna come to a Christmas party tomorrow?"

"What's this?" I answered, surprised at the invitation.

"The place I work gon' have a Christmas party tomorrow. Gon' be some real fine foxes there, some good whiskey, too," said Herman.

"Sure, I'll come. What time?"

"Meet me at 2:30 at _____, OK?"

"I'll be there," I said.

The men of the group continued to check us out. Herman was treating me as a friend, as an insider, as though my status in the group were somehow already assured. Certainly Herman would not invite just anyone to a party at work. Other group members wouldn't have expected this and in fact would have been surprised if he had asked one of them. After this demonstration by Herman, I could feel the others in the group warm up to me; they looked at me more directly and seemed to laugh more easily.

I began to feel comfortable enough to stand around in the group and listen to the banter, but not to participate in it, my reticence reflecting my sense of my visitor status. But I did laugh and talk with the fellows, trying to get to know people I had often wondered about during the past four or five weeks. These were people I had seen around but had never before attempted to "be with." After a while I told Herman and my new friends I had to be getting home.

For me the evening had been remarkable. It was the first time I had been introduced to anyone well connected within the social setting of Jelly's; the first time I had actually been sponsored by someone with an important social stake there. And no less significant, it was my first social venture on the liquor-store side of Jelly's—a real achievement. I had become involved with peer-group members, people for whom others at Jelly's really mattered. The whole experience marked the real beginning of my entree: It was the time from which I began to gain a feeling of place at Jelly's.

When Herman sponsored me and invited me to the party, I assumed some usefulness for and responsibility toward him. As I was to learn, one thing I could give Herman was verification of his role at the party— and of the identity that went along with it.

When I arrived at his place of work on the day of the party, Herman showed me around the buildings he kept clean as janitor. He led me from room to room, from hallway to hallway, and from floor to floor, taking great pride in their immaculate look. As he showed me around, he said in an aside that he would have to introduce me to others as his "cousin," since he could not let "just anybody" in there. I agreed to be his "cousin," which was still a dubious status in the minds of those we were to encounter at the party, if not in Herman's mind. But this was Herman's show. He was the director.

Before introducing me around Herman quietly asked me my mother's name. I told him. Then he told me his mother's name, and assured me all the while that this was "just in case somebody don't believe us." In exchanging our mothers' names, though, Herman and I demonstrated a certain degree of trust. Such confidential information is not generally disclosed to just anyone without reservation.

Another important point suggested by Herman's careful preparation of our story is that those at Jelly's who attempt a venturesome self-presentation have learned that they must expect to be seriously challenged. Hence they feel pressured to "have their shit together"—that is, to have a convincing and ready account of who they are. In the peer group at Jelly's this means that a person who expects to have his version of his identity taken seriously must have a "strong rap" (an impressive verbal account of himself) prepared, with good illustrations, details, and evidence.

In the world outside Jelly's—for example, at his place of work—Herman employs his own notions of what it takes to be believed, to be taken seriously, and to protect himself from being "shot down" or "blown away." These notions, grounded in Herman's experience on the streets around Jelly's, are the background to his careful preparation of our "story" for the people at the Christmas party.

At the party, Herman introduced me as his cousin who "goes to the University of Chicago, gettin' his Ph.D." He even told one black secretary that I was the cousin he had long been telling her about. Herman was the only janitor at the party; the others present were professionals and office workers. He and I were the only representatives from any setting at all like Jelly's. Yet with Herman's direction we moved easily among these people. With each introduction he beamed with pride over his "cousin, who's gettin' his Ph.D."

When the affair was over and we were leaving, Herman said to me, "I'm a man among men," declaring his own sense of accomplishment and self-esteem. Obviously, he felt that the whole show had been a great success. As we walked to my car, he repeated, "Yeah, I feel like a man among men. Eli, I knew you was a decent stud when I first met you. Now, you don't owe me nothing, you didn't have to come, but you came. You my best friend, hear?" Herman was elated at the success of his show and at how he had impressed the people "at work." As we were driving back to Jelly's Herman told me why he had chosen me to come to the party, rather than any of his buddies at Jelly's. "I wouldn't trust none o' them studs comin' all up on my job. Them cats don't know how to act 'round decent folks and intelligent folks. And sometimes I ain't so sure 'bout myself, 'specially if I get a little high on. Might get up there and start actin' a damn fool. Ha-ha." But Herman was sure about me. He was convinced that I knew how to act around "decent folks and intelligent folks." After all, I had "all that education." But equally important, I could come back and report to all the fellows at Jelly's, especially "ol' fat-assed Jelly" himself, about how we had partied with "decent folks at the Christmas party." He reminded me to do just that as he got out of my car.

When I did return to Jelly's, I told the fellows of the peer group how Herman and I had partied. With this verification of his story and, in a sense, of the identity he wanted them to know, I became all the more closely linked with him around Jelly's. All of this made a big hit there, and Herman's rank, at least when the outside world was the issue, became a little less precarious.

Group members seemed to accept my verification of Herman's adventures at work. Now when he spoke about "partying," people listened and were not as disparaging as they had been the day he invited me to the party. For the time being, at least to his face, the men seemed to have called a moratorium on attempting to "shoot him down" on this issue.

Thereafter Herman referred to me as his cousin and introduced me to others that way. In a sense this was the place I had lobbied for, however unwittingly. We hung together and treated each other as close friends, and the men followed suit. The more I hung with Herman and verified his stories, the closer we seemed to become. We began to "go for cousins," as the men say. Many of the men knew, of course, that we were not real cousins, and, perhaps even more important, Herman knew they knew. This was not a case of deception. Rather, the fictive kinship term of cousin was used by Herman, as it is by so many men on the streets around Jelly's, to signify that we were close friends.

One of the important implicit aspects of this developing relationship concerned its protective nature. Herman and I would often hang together and leave Jelly's together to go home or to a movie or somewhere else. Among peer-group members, an unspoken rule requires those who hang together to help or "take up for" one another in times of need— particularly during physical fights, but also on general social matters. My relationship with Herman gave me a certain implicit status in the group, a place interconnected with the "rep" and rank Herman was sensed to have. A set of mutual obligations and expectations began to form, so that group members expected us to take up for each other.

My growing awareness of these developments contributed to my own self-confidence around Jelly's liquor-store room, as I slowly secured a right to be there. During the course of this entree, I increasingly came under Herman's tutelage and guardianship. But why did Herman engage me in friendship at all? What was in it for him? After getting to know Herman better, I became aware that he regards himself as very knowledgeable about the ghetto streets. There is a certain amount of esteem to be gained by demonstrating that one knows his way around the streets, and Herman sees and presents himself as someone who has been "through it all."

Born and raised in Chicago, Herman has spent a good part of his life coming to terms with "the streets." He has been "through World War II," has been "a pimp, a hustler, a junkie" among other things—and has survived to talk about it all, something he does whenever "the streets" becomes an issue around Jelly's.

Because he carries this extensive and widely known personal biography, Herman is able to command a certain measure of esteem from the men who constitute Jelly's regular clientele. Other regulars usually agree with this definition of him and will work collectively to maintain it. At the same time, Herman wants to see himself as "decent." However, he knows that such an identity is difficult to maintain for anyone hanging out at Jelly's.

In our relationship I provided Herman with a kind of verification of his identity and status on the streets and in "decent" society. Specifically, as I provided him with a "decent" pupil, one who had "all that education," I reflected well upon him and could thus verify his own claims to "decency." Of course I could also verify Herman's claims to street prowess by allowing him to teach me about the streets. And this really was important to me, since I needed to know the streets if I were to survive and carry out my fieldwork. By taking me under his wing, Herman could show that he knew the streets very well and at the same time could "be somebody" when "decent" friends became the issue.

All this fit nicely with the low-key, nonassertive role I assumed at the beginning of my study. I behaved in this way to prevent unwieldy challenges from those who might have felt threatened by a more aggressive demeanor, especially from a stranger. It is the kind of role any outsider must play—is forced into—if he is not to disrupt the consensual definition of social order in this type of setting.

Carol Stack

Doing Research in The Flats

Carol Stack was one of the first social scientists to explore the functions of the kinship network in low-income communities. During the mid-1960s she conducted an extensive study of The Flats, the poorest section of a black community in the midwestern city of Jackson Harbor (both names are fictitious). Many of the residents had migrated to Jackson Harbor from the South in the 1930s and 1940s. Their hopes for a better life had been disappointed, and they had spent a lifetime in poverty. The same was true for their children and grandchildren.

Many of the residents of The Flats were unemployed, and most of those who were employed had low-paying service jobs and were not much better off than those who were eligible for welfare benefits. They lived in small, crowded, run-down wood-frame houses and shacks; the streets and yards were littered with broken glass, beer cans, and old cars.

Stack spent three years in close company with several women who lived in The Flats. She visited with them in their homes and accompanied them to clinics and welfare offices, day care centers, churches, and local markets. Gradually she became part of a "personal network" of friends in whose households she was welcome. In the course of her research she became intensely aware of the importance of such networks in the lives of the residents.

An important finding of Stack's research was that families in The Flats regarded many non-kin individuals as kin and included them in kinship-based exchange networks that linked together numerous domestic units. The community was also characterized by elastic household boundaries and lifelong bonds to three-generation households. These and other features of life in The Flats helped the residents adapt to a life of poverty, unemployment, and welfare dependency. In fact, Stack's report on her research, All Our Kin, *is subtitled* Strategies for Survival in a Black Community.

Like other researchers whose accounts are included in this volume, Stack faced the question of whether a white observer could ever be fully accepted in a black community. Eventually, as this selection shows, she was accepted—under the name of "white Caroline."

In both industrial and nonindustrial societies, researchers have typically established their first contacts with men who hold power—the colonial administrators, tribal chiefs, local mayors, and judges. These men draw upon their status in the community and favors owed to them to usher the researchers into the community, the first link in what becomes a chain of introductions. Anyone proceeding through other channels runs the risk of offending those in power and provoking an invitation to leave the community.

Within most black communities in the United States today, power is divided among the older generation of professionals in the black establishment and the younger activist leaders and organizations. I could have gained my first contacts in The Flats by working through the established network of black men and women who had status and power in The Flats and in the larger community of Jackson Harbor. In the mid-sixties two other white social scientists had entered the black community in Jackson Harbor through contacts with preachers, teachers, social workers, and other black professionals. Although they were not conducting a study requiring intensive participant-observer techniques, their research was confined and limited. They came into contact only with individuals and families chosen by the black establishment to represent the community: churchgoers, families on good terms with their social workers, and those men and women who had obtained legal marriages. Even more decisive as a handicap was their identification, in the eyes of those studied, with those black leaders who personally derived their status and importance from their acceptance within the white community. They were regarded as "uppity" individuals who "thought they were too good to sit down on an old couch."

When I first began this study in the mid-sixties, the community itself had produced a few articulate, intellectual spokesmen against racial and political injustice. Their speeches and their activities were aimed primarily at the white community. Within the black community itself, they were not controlling voices. I later came to know the young men and women involved in political activism within the black community as I became committed to their causes: a free health center, a Welfare Rights Organization, a job-training center, black businesses. Many of these individuals whom I met in the initial stages of this research later became members of activist organizations in The Flats. Such persons may, in the future, decide whether a research study of their community may be conducted and by whom. They may choose to censor findings that they believe may be used to repress, harm, or manipulate those studied.

Some of my colleagues strongly advised me to enter the black community through the older black establishment; they cited various reasons: Contacts were available; the research setting, they argued, was physically dangerous to a white person and I might need the sponsorship and protection that such contacts could provide; and tradition dictated such a procedure. I decided instead to find my own means of entree. I decided to circumvent the obvious centers of influence—the pastors, the politicians—and try to reach families without resorting to middlemen. Through my own efforts and good luck I came to know a young woman who had grown up on welfare in The Flats and had since come to my university. She agreed to introduce me to families she had known as she was growing up there. She would introduce me to two unrelated families and from then on I would be on my own.

In time I knew enough people well who were closely related so that after any family scene, gathering, or fight, I could put together interpretations of the events from the viewpoints of different individuals, particularly in instances when there were conflicts over rights in children. In addition to taking multiple observations of each event myself, I eventually asked others to assist me in the study. I found three Flats residents (two women and a man) who participated as part-time and casual assistants in the project. I selected individuals from the families I knew, who were interested in the study, and who were imaginative and critical thinkers. Together we worked out questions on various topics to ask the families studied.

We selected questions in the general areas of social and domestic relations, kinship and residence, and child-keeping; these questions provided a starting point for long discussions on a single issue. At no time did I formally interview anyone. I taped informal conversations after an event, when I was alone with someone I knew and with permission, asking that the situation be related to me from that person's point of view.

Because of the personal nature of the information obtained about individuals, and the promise that this information would be confidential, it was necessary to disguise the names of the informants. I gave a fictitious name to each person whose name or life entered into the study. Even when I tried out my own assumptions and interpretations of events on my friends and assistants, I used fictitious names for the examples.

The people that I studied in The Flats use first names in one another's presence, and to refer to their neighbors and friends. Surnames are used infrequently and often people do not know the surnames of long-time acquaintances and friends, although the coining of nicknames for siblings and friends is a creative and endless pastime. Nicknames personalize and endear; they dramatically expose memorable or striking characteristics about a person, giving him a very special identity. I also acquired several nicknames during the study, but the one that held was "white Caroline," a name originally given to me by a family to distinguish me from their niece whose name was also Caroline. (My real name, Carol, was always pronounced *Caroline*.) She became known as "black Caroline" soon after the children in her family began calling me "white Caroline." I first discovered this nickname one afternoon when I phoned the family and the youngster who answered the phone called out, "Mama, white Caroline's on the phone."

Members of a culture have biases that affect their perceptions of themselves and their life ways; outsiders bring biases to the cultures they study. Although life experiences produce a difference in perceptions, these perceptions can be shared. The three years I spent in The Flats opened and reassembled my life ways and my understanding of womanhood, parenthood, and the American economy. Likewise, I brought perceptions and biases to the study that joggled and molded the views of those closest to me.

A researcher in the social sciences is practically always defined as an outsider in a study, even if he or she has close attachment and commitment to the community, and shares a similar cultural background. Even a study of the culture of one's most intimate associations—our friends, colleagues, or kin—thrusts the researcher apart. Whether studying elites, bureaucracy, or the poor, if one hopes to discover the rules of routine behavior, the observer himself must attempt to learn how to move appropriately inside the private world of those observed. The researcher must take time and patience and practice, attempting to reduce the distance between the model outsiders used to explain social order and the explanations employed by those studied. Attempts will fail, but this prodding hopefully will bring the observer to an intimate point of contact in the study whereby he becomes both an actor and a subject whose learned definitions can themselves be analyzed.

An important stage of my research began when my car broke down. Despite the fact that the car was a convenience—it gave me an easily explainable role in the lives of the families I knew, helping me provide daily assistance with the children, the shopping, the problems with "papers,'' the welfare office, sick children, and so on—when it broke down I decided not to fix it. Without the car, my presence in the community was less apparent. I was able to spend long days in the homes of people I had met, participating in their daily lives. I had already developed tentative hypotheses on the style of social relations in The Flats and on the ways in which people expand their network of exchange. I began to focus my attention on how networks were expanded, who the participants were, and how residents in The Flats see and interpret this process.

My role in the community at this point was no longer that of an outsider. To many families I became another link in the systems of exchanges that were part of their existence. Viola Jackson's sisters once told me that people look at you when you have a white friend, saying that you are really on the white man's side and that you do everything they want you to do. But Ophelia said to me that people understand what friendship means. Friends can ask any favor of one another, any time of the night, and it shouldn't make any difference. No one would tell you to drop a friend you can trust even if she is white. Ruby Banks told me that from the first day we started going around together, people said that we looked alike and that we did so much together that we seemed just ''like sisters.'' Our affinity influenced the behavior of Ruby's kin toward me and their persistent concern for my well-being. It also influenced Ruby's behavior toward me in public settings within and outside the ghetto. When Ruby's youngest child was sick in the local hospital, we went to visit her. The first day, the white nurse on duty stopped me—the rules stated that only close relatives could visit. Ruby told the nurse angrily, ''Caroline here is my sister, and nothing's stopping her from visiting this baby.'' Ruby's claim went unchallenged, and we were able to visit the baby every day.

Terry Williams

Exploring the Cocaine Culture

Terry Williams is a young African-American sociologist who specializes in ethnographic research. He has investigated the hopes and dreams of unemployed teenagers, the interactions of proprietors and patrons in pornography establishments, and the subculture of cocaine users in after-hours clubs. It is the latter research that forms the subject of this selection.

A guiding principle of Williams's research is the desire to take the insider's point of view rather than approaching his subject with the pre-conceived ideas of an outsider. In order to see the world through the eyes of the insider, he must become intimate with the people he is observing. In fact, he becomes part of their life; they are no longer "subjects" or informants but friends and associates.

Williams was relatively inexperienced when he undertook his study of the cocaine culture, and he learned many lessons the hard way. Especially troublesome were the ethical implications of the research—whether he had a right to observe individuals engaging in a private (and illegal) activity, and whether his role as a reporter of those activities would later create problems for those who trusted him with privileged information. There was also the matter of risk: There can be no doubt that Williams was in considerable danger on several occasions while conducting his study.

One outcome of Williams's research in the after-hours clubs was that it led to further research on cocaine use. In the 1970s he became aware of a new way of using the drug, known as free-basing, which turned out to be a precursor of the "crack" epidemic of recent years. Thus, al-though The Blue Cat Cafe *was never published, Williams went on to write* The Cocaine Kids, *which was published by Addison-Wesley in 1989. The latter work includes what Williams calls "dramatic portraits" of young cocaine dealers that portray the "kids" as they see themselves.*

The following account contains several illustrations of the process through which Williams learned how to locate and interact with mem-bers of the cocaine users' subculture.

In 1974, after completing serveral years of graduate study in sociology at the City University of New York, I accepted a teaching position at John Jay College of Criminal Justice. My first assignment entailed com-muting from the main campus to Rikers Island to teach in the satellite program established by the college. After a year in this special program, I became friendly with several of the inmates, many of whom were serv-ing relatively light sentences. Upon their release, three of them called me and offered to take me out on the town.

They showed me the nightlife of New York City as I had never seen it before. In small, intimate clubs known as after-hours spots, I was introduced to a bewildering variety of people—musicians, drug dealers, punk rockers, transvestites, secretaries, doctors, dancers, gamblers, ac-tors, policemen, prostitutes—all of whom were there to share in a life-style based on the enjoyment of cocaine and the pleasure and excitement brought on by the intensity of their interaction. I mentioned this experi-ence to some of my colleagues and mentors at the CUNY Graduate Cen-ter, and they encouraged me to conduct a systematic study of cocaine use in after-hours clubs.

On a few occasions early in my research I traveled alone through for-bidding city streets in the hope of gaining entry to a club on my own. But the clubs are private enterprises with a distinctive clientele. Among other things, dress is an important criterion in establishing membership; time after time I was denied entry because I lacked the proper attire. I needed to wear leather, suede, or other elegant clothing, and avoid the collegiate look. Since I could not afford these accoutrements, I adopted the strategy of giving a name or nickname that is fairly commonly used by patrons of after-hours clubs, such as Iceman, Cool Breeze, Mr. T, Jack, Slick, or Country. There are always people with names like these in the community of hustlers. Sometimes I gave the name of a person I knew to be a member of a particular club, and occasionally this strategy worked, but many times it did not.

On those occasions when I succeeded in gaining entry to a club, I made an effort to become acquainted with the doorman, barmaids, and patrons. After eight months in the field, I became friendly with the doorman at a club in midtown Manhattan. It turned out that he knew dozens of people in clubs throughout the city. His name became my password; it guaranteed entry into his club (when he was not working there) and several others.

Getting into the clubs did not automatically give me access to a new set of contacts; quite the contrary. I had to be especially careful not to appear overly friendly or curious, yet I knew that direct experiential involvement with key members of the clubs was essential. I knew that building rapport was the single most important dynamic in an otherwise difficult social world. I knew, too, that I must interact with at least one person who attended the club on a regular basis. I had to become something more than an observer; otherwise I would be under the continual scrutiny of owner/managers and many of the patrons.

To accomplish this goal I had to identify something within the cocaine culture that would allow me to interact with club members without using cocaine. I observed several patrons actually refusing cocaine that was offered them, saying "my nose is out" or "I'm coked out" or simply that they did not trust other people's drugs. Using this technique, which fit the norms of the subculture I was observing, allowed me to interact without attracting suspicion and at the same time to gain a measure of unanticipated respect from dealers who felt that many patrons took advantage of the ceremonial offering of cocaine and became "overindulgers" or "vacuum cleaner sniffers."

In this way I became a participant observer of cocaine users in after-hours clubs. As a patron of the clubs, I could observe how people use cocaine in their face-to-face relations with others. There being no standard rules for a study of this nature, I had to establish several for myself. They were as follows:

1. Avoid using all drugs.
2. Establish solid rapport with key persons.
3. Avoid pretension, be yourself.
4. Ask people what names they give themselves (e.g., cokehead, player, businessman, dealer).
5. Do not label indiscriminately or stereotype.
6. Do not betray the trust of your contacts.

Even with these rules, my research was plagued with problems of ethics as well as some very real dangers. I had no illusions about the dangers of research on drug users and was then, as I am now, concerned about the possible legal and legislative consequences of this kind of research. I drew some (but not much) consolation from the realization that people have been using cocaine and gathering in after-hours clubs for over a century and will probably continue to do so even in the face of legal and other obstacles.

Some of the ramifications of research of this kind became evident on two occasions, one past and one recent. The recent occasion involved a trial in which I was an expert witness and was asked to name one of my informants, a major heroin and cocaine dealer. I refused and was held in contempt of court by a federal judge. I was not remanded to jail because I produced a letter of confidentiality that essentially made my notes and contacts immune from prosecution by virtue of their anonymity.

In the earlier instance, I was in a Brooklyn club where I was already conspicuous as a nonuser of cocaine. It seems that I was also overzealous, in the sense that I was staring too much and asking too many questions. One of the club's owners came over to me and said, "Listen, my man, if you're undercover, I got people that'll take care of that." I was not sure whether he meant force or bribery, but in any case I stopped going to that club.

On another occasion I was in a club that had been heterosexual until the Thursday night I arrived, which was "gay night." I thought I would take advantage of the situation for sociological purposes, making comparisons between heterosexual and homosexual cocaine users. I was wearing black leather (the fashion in New York at the time), not realizing the role of black leather in the gay community. I noticed a group of men sitting in a corner and moved toward them inconspicuously, or so I thought, until I was eight or ten feet away. One of them stared up at me and I of course looked toward him. His sleeves were rolled past his elbows, revealing purple and red tattoos on both arms. After looking at me for a few seconds, he walked over and offered to buy me a drink, asking if this was my first time there. I explained that I had been there before and informed him that I was a researcher and just wanted to talk to as many people as possible. He grew red in the face and said to his companions in a loud voice, hands on hips, head cocked to one side, "Hey, get a load of this one. He wants to do research on us. You scum bag! What do we look like, pal? Fucking guinea pigs? You got some nerve walking in here, talking about doing some research!"

By this time everyone in the place was staring at me and I was embarrassed and a bit shaken up by the turn of events. I went over to the bar and the bartender said to me, "Don't mind Wayne, he's off duty [a policeman] and likes to throw his weight around."

It was at times like these that I seriously questioned facets of my methodological approach. This was only one of many such incidents (which fortunately never became violent) that occurred during my initial fieldwork. It did not take me long to realize that this approach would not work. I then decided to be selective in informing people of my purpose; I would inform others about my findings after the research was completed. This plan has been all but impossible to carry out. Many of the clubs I visited have either closed or moved to new locations unknown to me. Many of the patrons have moved on; some have died; others have gone to prison. The after-hours club has a transient quality that I was not aware of at the beginning of my study.

My observations of cocaine users in clubs suggested that the dealers who supply them with the drug are as significant as the club itself. Although the clubs' managers often sold cocaine to patrons, most users obtained their cocaine from dealers outside the clubs so that they could give it away inside in the ritual sharing snorters engage in. Therefore, to supplement my understanding of the cocaine culture in the after-hours clubs, I conducted interviews with a number of dealers. Many dealers were unwilling to act as contacts because they feared that I would be unable to guarantee confidentiality. Nevertheless, there were some who had a story to tell, and I was there to listen.

As a researcher, I knew what data I needed: information on cocaine users and the associated nightlife, street myths about use and pharmacology, emerging trends, and other elements of cultural lore. But as most researchers know, there is a quid pro quo in every research situation. What the researcher wants is not always what the contact desires in exchange. I was asked to do a variety of favors, such as lending money and finding lawyers, social workers, doctors, painters, apartments, caterers, and clothing stores. On many occasions I was asked to engage in illegal acts. The most memorable of those occurred when I was at the home of a dealer whom I will call Alfredo. The phone rang and Alfredo had a heated argument with the caller. After hanging up, he waited a few choice seconds, then looked me in the eye and said, "Listen, a guy is coming over here and I owe him money. He wants what I owe him in coke. I told him I didn't have any blow [cocaine], but somebody told him I did. Now I told him my friend is here and he has some, but it's expensive. All I want you to do is hold this bag [it contained about 2 ounces of cocaine], and when he comes tell him it's yours and it'll cost him $1,500—no more, no less. Don't bat an eyelash no matter what he does or says."

Before I could say anything, the doorbell rang and a friend of Alfredo's whom I had met previously arrived. They both started to laugh, saying that the whole episode had been a joke for the purposes of testing me.

This and similar requests put me in an awkward position, and I have often thought about this as if it were not a joke. What if there really had been someone to whom Alfredo owed money—a situation that occurred frequently in his life as a dealer—and that person knew the kinds of games Alfredo played? There are many "what if's" in this type of research. Yet even though I felt that it was inappropriate—not to mention illegal and dangerous—to perform such services, I could not refuse what appeared to Alfredo to be a simple favor—especially after he had given me access to information that could send him to jail for life.

This kind of research, in which one both observes and becomes part of the group under study, is called ethnography, participant observation, qualitative research, or field study by social scientists, and advanced journalism by their critics. Ethnography is the science of cultural description; more than that, it is a methodology. It is a way of looking at people, a way of looking at a culture. It is recording how people perceive, construct, and interact in their own private world. It embraces the subjective reality of the individuals it seeks to understand. It defines the group the way the group defines itself.

But cocaine use, because it is illegal, cannot be examined in isolation from the society in which it occurs. Every sniff of cocaine is an act of rebellion, an act performed in defiance of the the law. The hidden dissent of cocaine users, and of drug dealers more generally, is just one aspect of the symbolic dissent in which many Americans are participating in the late twentieth century. The corporate executive, the coffee shop owner, the fashion designer, the corrupt police officer, the restaurant owner—all evade taxes, use illegal drugs, and beat the system in one way or another. The interactions of individuals in cocaine clubs, thus, are part of a larger mosaic that includes such forces as class conflict and social control.

Within this context, I explored the night-time world of cocaine users with scholarly interest. In the hundreds of hours I spent in after-hours clubs I was able to discover, penetrate, and examine this world with few distractions. I became acquainted with the after-hours life of fear, risk, desire, disapproval, and revolt. I sought to grasp it, to touch even its more dangerous side. At the same time, I was standing outside of this secret world, counting and categorizing, measuring and comparing. I was trying to understand the cocaine culture without becoming absorbed by it.

Part II

Building Relationships

Despite the barriers we were able to look at each other, walk along-side each other, talk, and occasionally touch fingers. When two people stand up close to [a chain-link] fence on either side, without touching it, they can look through the interstices and forget that they are looking through a fence.

Elliot Liebow

Elliot Liebow

A Field Experience
in Retrospect

Elliot Liebow's study of a group of black men who hung out on a street corner in Washington, D.C., in the early 1960s has become a classic of the anthropological and sociological literature. Liebow's purpose was to record and interpret the everyday life of lower-class black males "on their grounds and on their terms." In order to accomplish this he became part of a shifting collection of men who came together more or less regularly on a sidewalk in a blighted section of downtown Washington. His book Tally's Corner *is a sensitive, insightful portrayal of the highly circumscribed yet unexpectedly complex lives of those men.*

The New Deal Carry-out Shop, where Liebow spent much of his time as a participant observer, was located in the Second Precinct, a section of Washington that was known for its high rates of poverty, crime, and social dependency. The shop served not only as a place to obtain prepared food but also as a neighborhood communication center and as a staging area for a variety of activities both legal and illegal. The men who frequented the store and the sidewalk outside were construction workers, day laborers, menial workers in service trades, or unemployed. They lacked education, skills, and earning power; in short, they were "losers" and knew it. Liebow became one of them.

Liebow spent a year and a half observing and recording the daily routines of about two dozen men as they moved around the immediate neighborhood of the Carry-out Shop. He joined them on the street and in the alleys, in poolrooms and beer joints, and in their homes. In the course of his research he discovered how resourceful and resilient they could be despite the apparent disorganization and insecurity of their lives. He also discovered how important friendship was to these men. For them, friendship was almost the only source of self-esteem; it also served as a buffer between them and an incredibly stressful environment.

Liebow himself became a friend of the men who hung out on Tally's Corner. He was welcomed into their homes and into their lives. But he could not help being different—not only in race but in income, education, and temperament. A year after he had begun his research Liebow wrote: "The wall between us remained, or better, the chain-link fence, since despite the barriers we were able to look at each other, walk alongside each other, talk, and occasionally touch fingers."

In the following pages Liebow describes his efforts to come to terms with the differences between himself and the men on Tally's Corner.

In taking up the project director's suggestion that this would be "a good place to get your feet wet," I went in so deep that I was completely submerged and my plan to do three or four separate studies, each with its own neat, clean boundaries, dropped forever out of sight. My initial excursions into the street—to poke around, get the feel of things, and to lay out the lines of my fieldwork—seldom carried me more than a block or two from the corner where I started. From the very first weeks or even days, I found myself in the middle of things; the principal lines of my fieldwork were laid out, almost without my being aware of it. For the next year or so, and intermittently thereafter, my base of operations was the corner Carry-out across the street from my starting point.

The first time out, I had gone less than one short block when I noticed a commotion up the street. A man—Detective Wesley, I learned later—was dragging a kicking, screaming woman to a police call box. A small crowd had gathered on each of the four corners to watch. I approached two men and asked what the woman had done. Both were uncertain. The younger of the two said that he had heard two stories and proceeded to tell me both of them, concluding with the observation that he had known Detective Wesley for six or seven years and that he was "nobody to fool with."

I said that sometimes being a cop seems to do something to a man. This led to a discussion of policemen and each of us contributed personal experiences or anecdotes on the subject. After ten or fifteen minutes of this, the older man said goodbye and walked off. The younger man stayed on. Across the street from where we were standing was the Downtown Cafe. I suggested that we go in and have some coffee and he agreed. As we walked across the street he asked if I was a policeman. I told him no and explained that I was working on a study of family life in the city. There was no more discussion about who I was or why I was there. We sat at the bar for several hours talking over coffee.

I had not accomplished what I set out to do, but this was only the first day. And, anyway, when I wrote up this experience that evening, I felt that it presented a fairly good picture of this young man and that most of the material was to the point. Tomorrow, I decided, I would go back to my original plan—nothing had been lost.

But tomorrow never came. At nine the next morning, I headed down the same street. Four men were standing in a group in front of the Carry-out. Three were winos, in their forties—all marked with old scars on face and neck, dressed shabbily, but sober. The fourth was a man of 32 or 33, who looked as if he had just stepped out of a slick magazine advertisement. One of the winos had a month-old puppy stuck in the front of his overcoat. Only the dog's head was exposed.

The group approached me and one of the older men said, "Isn't he a nice puppy?" I said yes, and began patting the dog. "He just bought him," one man said. The puppy was whining. "Maybe it's hungry," said the older man, "let's get him some hamburger." "No man, he'll get worms from that stuff," said one of the others. I suggested milk and we all went into the Carry-out. I asked the waitress for a half pint of milk. The man asked for a saucer. "You can't feed him here," the waitress said, "the Health Department would close us up." She gave us a paper plate and the milk (paid for by me). We took the dog into a hallway next door. Everyone was pleased at how eagerly the puppy drank.

A man who had been in the Carry-out joined us in the hallway. "That's a shepherd, isn't he? Just what I want for my little boy." I said, "I wish I could get one for my little girl, but she's allergic to all animals, dust, and lots of things." "It's better that way," said one of the winos. "She'll outgrow it. But man, if you don't have that until you're full grown—man, look out." "Yes, that's right," the newcomer agreed. "I know a woman who got allergies after she was grown and she got bronica asthma with it."

The dog finished the milk. The owner put him back in his overcoat and I shook hands all around with the winos. We split up three ways. The winos went up the street, the well-dressed man down the street, and the newcomer—who turned out to be Tally Jackson—and I went into the Carry-out.

For more than four hours Tally and I lounged around in the Carry-out, talking, drinking coffee, watching people come in and go out, watching other hangers-on as they bantered with the waitresses, horsed around among themselves, or danced to the jukebox. Everyone knew Tally and some frequently sought out his attention. Tally sometimes participated in the banter but we were generally left undisturbed when we were talking. When I left at two o'clock, Tally and I were addressing each other by first names ("Elliot" was strange to him and we settled for "Ellix") and I was able to address the two waitresses by their first names without feeling uncomfortable. I had also learned to identify several other men by their first names or nicknames, had gotten hints on personal relationships, and had a biographical sketch (part of it untrue, I learned later) of Tally.

Back on the street, I ended up at the Downtown Cafe, this time by way of the morning's now very drunk owner of the puppy, who was standing near the entrance. The puppy was our bond and we talked about him with an enthusiasm that perhaps neither of us felt. Later, the well-dressed man who had also been part of the puppy episode came in and joined me at the bar. Then, still drinking beer at the bar, I met two other men in quick succession. The first man had to leave shortly for his night-shift busboy job at the restaurant. The other was a surly man in his middle thirties who initiated the contact by taking the stool next to me and asking what kind of work I did, adding that he had seen me around the day before, watching Detective Wesley drag that woman across the street.

I told him briefly what my job was.

"Well, if you hang around here you'll see it all. Anything can happen and it does happen here. It can get rough and you can get your head knocked in. You'll be OK though, if you know one or two of the right people."

"That's good to know," I told him, guessing (and hoping) that he was one of the "right people." He left me with the impression that he was being friendly and, in a left-handed sort of way, was offering me his protection.

By the end of the second day I had met nine men, learned the names of several more, and spent many hours in close public association with several men, at least two of whom were well known. And perhaps most important of all, in my own mind I had partly sloughed off that feeling of being a stranger and achieved that minimum sense of "belonging" which alone permits an ease of manner and mind so essential in building personal relationships.

Over the next three or four weeks, I made several excursions into other neighborhoods and followed up at the Downtown Cafe and the Carry-out shop on an irregular basis, getting to know some of the people better and many others for the first time. Frequently I ate breakfast and lunch at the Carry-out and began putting occasional dimes in the juke-box and in the pinball machine. Ted Moore, who worked at a liquor store nearby and whom I had first met in the Carry-out while he was waiting for the store to open, regularly alternated with me in buying coffee and doughnuts in the morning. At the Downtown Cafe the man who told me that I'd be OK if I knew "one or two of the right people" publicly identified me as his friend. ("Sure I know him," he told another man in my presence. "We had a long talk the other day. He's my friend and he's OK, man, he's OK. At first I thought he was a cop, but he's no cop. He's OK.")

All in all, I felt I was making steady progress. There was still plenty of suspicion and mistrust, however. At least two men who hung around the Carry-out—one of them the local numbers man—had seen me dozens of times in close quarters, but they kept their distance and I kept mine. Once, accidentally, I caught the numbers man's eye as I walked in. We held the stare for three or four seconds and I nodded slightly but he wouldn't let go. I went on about my business, determined that I wasn't going to be stared down next time and that he'd get no more nods from me unless he nodded first. As it turned out, I didn't have long to wait.

One mid-February day, I walked into the Carry-out. Tally was having a cup of coffee. "Look here," he said. "Where is this place?" Tally took out a sheet of paper from an envelope and handed it to me. It was a summons to appear as a witness for the defense in the case of the United States versus Lonny Reginald Small. A faint stamp indicated that Tally was to report to the United States District Court for the District of Columbia at 3rd and Pennsylvania Avenue, Northwest, at ten o'clock this morning. I read off the address. It was then 9:40. I suggested that he take a cab, but when he said he didn't have the money I offered to drive him down. He quickly accepted. On the way, he explained that Lonny was a friend of his. Lonny was being tried for murdering his wife last summer. "Lonny is a nice guy," he said. "He's one hundred percent."

Thus began a three-week odyssey into the world of Lonny Small, a young man of 26 who, according to the jury's subsequent verdict of "not guilty," had choked his wife to death accidentally. Upon his acquittal, Lonny was rearrested in the courthouse for a violation of probation (on a previous grand larceny conviction) in another jurisdiction. He waived extradition, was given a hearing, was released on an appearance bond, and after another hearing he was again placed on probation.

Almost imperceptibly, my association with Tally, and through him with Lonny, was projecting me into the role of a principal actor in Lonny's life. By being with Tally through the trial, I found that first Tally, then Lonny, were looking to me for leadership and, as in the question of waiving extradition, for decision making. Court officials, apparently taking their cues from Lonny, began looking to me as his spokesman.

The follow-up of Lonny, which took most of my time for at least the next two weeks, carried me into dozens of places and into contact with scores of people. Throughout this period I stayed in close touch with the project director, getting clearance for and weighing the possible consequences of my growing involvement with the authorities. I went to three different jails during this time, sat through one murder trial and two hearings in judges' chambers, testifying at one of them. I went to bondsmen's offices, to the United States Employment Service, to the Blessed Martin de Porres Hostel (for homeless men), and into several private homes. I met policemen, judges, lawyers, bondsmen, probation officers, and one of Lonny's former employers. I talked with his friends and at least one enemy, his mother-in-law, whose daughter he had killed. I met in council several times with various members of his extended family (who accepted me, through Tally, as Lonny's friend, no questions asked) in their houses, and drove around with them to the houses of other members of the family trying to raise money for Lonny's bond.

Meanwhile, back at the Carry-out, where Tally and I were meeting regularly at night and where I tried to stop in during the day whenever possible, people I had never seen, or others I had seen but never spoken to, began coming up to me and asking, "Is Lonny out yet?" or "Did you raise his bail yet?" or simply, "How's it going?" Bumdoodle, the numbers man, one of those who had not known Lonny, was especially solicitous of Lonny's welfare. He, too, began calling me by my first name and, although I kept no record of it, I think it was at this time that he dropped all subterfuge in taking numbers in my presence and soon began taking bets from me.

By the middle of March, Tally and I were close friends ("up tight") and I was to let him know if I wanted or needed "anything, anytime." By April, the number of men whom I had come to know fairly well and their acceptance of me had reached the point at which I was free to go to the rooms or apartments where they lived or hung out, at almost any time, needing neither an excuse nor an explanation for doing so. Like other friends, I was there to pass the time, to hang around, to find out "what's happening."

I switched my day around to coincide with the day worker's leisure hours: from four in the afternoon until late at night, according to what was going on. Alone, or with one, two, or half a dozen others, I went to poolrooms, to bars, or to somebody's room or apartment. Much of the time we just hung around the Carry-out, playing the pinball machine or standing on the corner watching the world go by. Regularly at five, I met my five "drinking buddies" when they came off from work and we went into a hallway for an hour or so of good drinking and easy talk.

Friday afternoon to Sunday night was especially exciting and productive. I'd go to Nancy's "place" (apartment) where, at almost any hour, one could get liquor, listen to music, or engage in conversation. Or perhaps seven or eight of us would buy some beer and whiskey and go up to Tonk's apartment near the Carry-out where he lived with his wife.

Occasionally, I'd pair up with one or two men and go to a party, a movie, or a crap game, which might be in almost any part of town. Sunday afternoon was an especially good time to pick up news or happenings of the preceding 48 hours. People were generally rested up from the night before, relaxed, and ready to fill one another in on events which involved the police, breakups of husband-wife relations and bed-and-board arrangements, drink-stimulated brawls, sex adventures, and parties they had witnessed, heard about, or participated in over Friday and Saturday.

By April most people seemed to be taking it for granted that I belonged in the area. At least two men did not trust me or like me, but by then I was too strongly entrenched for them to challenge successfully my right to be there, even had they chosen to do so. New people moved into the area and I found myself being regarded as an old-timer, sometimes being asked to corroborate events which predated my arrival.

Throughout this period, my field observations were focused on individuals: what they said, what they did, and the contexts in which they said them or did them. I sought them out and was sought out by them.

My field notes contain a record of what I saw when I looked at Tally, Richard, Sea Cat, and the others. I have only a small notion—and one that I myself consider suspect—of what they saw when they looked at me.

Some things, however, are very clear. They saw, first of all, a white man. In my opinion, this brute fact of color, as they understood it in their experience and as I understood it in mine, irrevocably and absolutely relegated me to the status of outsider. I am not certain, but I have a hunch that they were more continuously aware of the color difference than I was. When four of us sat around a kitchen table, for example, I saw three Negroes; each of them saw two Negroes and a white man.

Sometimes, when the word "nigger" was being used easily and conversationally or when, standing on the corner with several men, one would have a few words with a white passerby and call him a "white mother-fucker," I used to play with the idea that maybe I wasn't as much of an outsider as I thought. Other events, and later readings of the field materials, have disabused me of this particular touch of vanity.

Whenever the fact of my being white was openly introduced, it pointed up the distance between me and the other person, even when the intent of introducing it was, I believe, to narrow that distance. On one occasion, for example, all of us left Tally's room together. Tally grabbed my arm and pulled me aside near the storefront church and said, "I want to talk to you." With no further introduction, he looked me straight in the eye and started talking.

"I'm a liar. I been lying to you all along now and I want to set it straight, even if it means we can't be friends no more. I only lied to you about one thing. Everything else I told you is gospel truth but I did lie about one thing and that makes me a liar. I know that some white people think that if you catch a man in a lie one time you can't never trust him after that. And even if you feel that way about it I still got to tell you. You remember when you first came around here, I told you . . . Well, that was a lie. . . . I didn't think nothing of it at first, but then you and me started going around together and when we started getting real tight, my conscience started whomping me. I kept looking for a place to tell you but it never seemed right. Then tonight . . . I knew this was the right time. I knew you were going to find out and I didn't want you to find out from somebody else.''

Once I was with Richard in his hometown. It was his first visit in five years. We arrived in the middle of the night and had to leave before daybreak because Richard was wanted by the local police. We were in his grandmother's house. Besides Richard, there were his grandmother, his aunt, and two unrelated men, both long-time friends of Richard.

The group was discussing the possibility of Richard's coming home to stay and weighing the possible consequences. In the middle of the discussion, Richard interrupted and nodded at me. "Now Ellix here is white, as you can see, but he's one of my best friends. Him and me are real tight. You can say anything you want, right to his face. He's real nice." "Well," said his Aunt Pearl, "I always did say there are some nice white people."

Whether or not there is more to these citations than "Some of my best friends are . . ." or "Yes, but you're different," the wall between us remained, or better, the chain-link fence, since despite the barriers we were able to look at each other, walk alongside each other, talk, and occasionally touch fingers. When two people stand up close to the fence on either side, without touching it, they can look through the interstices and forget that they are looking through a fence.

The disadvantage of being white was offset in part by the fact that, as an outsider, I was not a competitor. Thus, in the matter of skin color, I saw myself nowhere in the spectrum of black- to light-skinned (or "bright"); I was completely out of it, with no vested interest. Looking at me, however, the people I came to know in the area probably saw more than a "white male adult." They saw or knew many other things as well, any one of which relegated me to outside status. Those with whom I was in regular contact knew, for example, that I was with them because it was my job to be with them, and they knew, according to their individual comprehension and my ability to communicate, just what my job was. They knew that I lived outside the area. They knew that I was a college graduate, or at least they associated an advanced education with the work I was doing. Moreover, it was apparent, certainly to me, that I was not fluent in their language. Thus, I was an outsider not only because of race, but also because of occupation, education, residence, and speech. The fact that I was Jewish came up only twice. Once, a man who worked but did not live in the area threw some Yiddish expressions at me because "I thought you looked Jewish." The other time was when I met a soldier in a local bootleg joint. We had been talking for some ten minutes or so when he asked me whether I was "Eyetalian." I told him I was Jewish. "That's just as good," he said. "I'm glad you're not white."

The fact that I was married and a father, and that I was bigger than average size—6'1", 185 pounds—probably didn't matter much, except as they entered incidentally into my personal relationship with one or another individual. Since the people I spent most of my time with ranged in age from 20 to the middle forties, I would guess that my age (37) was not significant in itself.

I was an outsider on several different counts. From the outset, I had decided that I would never shoot crap, pool, or play cards for money, or bet money in any way (numbers excepted, since playing numbers is safely impersonal), and would meticulously avoid the slightest suspicion of a personal involvement with any women. These self-imposed restrictions to some extent did underline my marginality. My explanation that I couldn't afford to chance a fight or bad feelings because of my job was usually accepted and I was generally excused from participating in these activities rather than excluded from them.

But although I was an outsider, I also was a participant in a full sense of the word. The people I was observing knew that I was observing them, yet they allowed me to participate in their activities and take part in their lives to a degree that continues to surprise me. Some "exploited" me, not as an outsider but rather as one who, as a rule, had more resources than they did. When one of them came up with the resources—money or a car, for example—he too was "exploited" in the same way. I usually tried to limit money or other favors to what I thought each would have gotten from another friend had he the same resources as I. I tried to meet requests as best I could without becoming conspicuous. I was not always on the giving end and learned somewhat too slowly to accept food or let myself be treated to drinks even though I knew this would work a hardship on the giver.

When in the field, I participated as fully and as whole-mindedly as I could, limited only by my own sense of personal and professional propriety and by what I assumed to be the boundaries of acceptable behavior as seen by those I was with.

Occasionally, when I wanted to record a physical description of, say, a neighborhood, an apartment, or a social event, I tried to be an observer only. In practice, I found it impossible to keep all traces of participation out of a straight observer role.

One Saturday night, with my observer role clearly in mind, I went to a dance at the Capitol Arena where more than a thousand people were jammed together. I was the only white male, this was my first time at such an event, the music was so foreign to me that I picked out the wrong beat, and I was unable to identify several of the band instruments. I was, willy-nilly, an observer. But it was very hot, it was very noisy, it was very smelly, and it was all very exciting. It was impossible to remain simply an observer in a place like this, even for someone as phlegmatic as I. It was only a few minutes after Jackie Wilson started singing that I discovered that the noise wasn't nearly loud enough, the heat wasn't nearly hot enough, and the odor from more than a thousand closely packed people was not really strong enough at all. Like everyone else, I wanted more of everything.

Almost from the beginning, I adopted the dress and something of the speech of the people with whom I was in most frequent contact, as best I could without looking silly or feeling uncomfortable. I came close in dress (in warm weather, tee or sport shirt and khakis or other slacks) with almost no effort at all. My vocabulary and diction changed, but not radically. Cursing and using ungrammatical constructions at times—though they came easily—did not make any of my adaptations confusable with the speech of the street. Thus, while remaining conspicuous in speech and perhaps in dress, I had dulled some of the characteristics of my background. I probably made myself more accessible to others, and certainly more acceptable to myself. This last point was forcefully brought home to me one evening when, on my way to a professional meeting, I stopped off at the Carry-out in a suit and tie. My loss of ease made me clearly aware that the change in dress, speech, and general carriage was as important for its effect on me as it was for its effect on others.

In retrospect, it seems as if the degree to which one becomes a participant is as much a matter of perceiving oneself as a participant as it is of being accepted as a participant by others.

Ruth Horowitz

Getting In

In the early 1970s Ruth Horowitz conducted extensive field research among the Chicano residents of the 32nd Street neighborhood in Chicago. In the course of her research she became fascinated by the contradictions she observed in their behavior. She saw residents making great efforts to help one another, both financially and socially. At the same time, young men were shot on street corners while discussing ways of making peace among rival gangs. Residents demonstrated for better educational opportunities, yet the schools were discouraging and dangerous places. "The cultural life of this Chicago community," Horowitz wrote, "is organized around several pivotal themes: violence and convention, public life and private identity, honor and the American dream . . ."

To better understand this broad cultural pattern, Horowitz focused on teenagers as they interacted and developed identities in various social settings. She also examined the process through which young people make the transition from teenager to older community member. Her research highlighted the continual tension between the individualistic suc-

cess ethic, as taught and expected in the schools and on the job, and the collective solidarity of the peer group.

Young people in this community carved out several distinctive life-styles. Some young men were immersed in the social world of fighting gangs; others remained on the periphery, sometimes becoming involved in fights but generally only responding to what they perceived as insults rather than instigating incidents (a way to enhance a gang member's reputation). Other youth rigorously avoided the world of the streets and concentrated on getting an education or holding a job. But while their orientations to the street world were distinct, all the youth interacted with one another.

The young women moved in social worlds that were largely separate from those of the men. Most of them experienced tension in the realm of sexuality and motherhood. Only a few oriented their lives toward a work career. The others developed several strategies for resolving the dilemma between the importance of remaining a virgin and the need to give in to the sexual demands of a boyfriend.

Horowitz's research goals required that she spend a great deal of time with the teenage residents of 32nd Street as well as with families living in the community. She also observed residents in the schools, at political meetings, at dances and parties, and in the streets. For much of the time she hung out with the members of fighting gangs on street corners, in parks, and sometimes in their homes. She did not become a gang member; instead, she became accepted as a sort of reporter; some of the teenagers dubbed her "Lois Lane." But while her entry into the community and the lives of its residents was relatively easy, after a year she found that residents increasingly defined her in terms of local community expectations, creating problems for her as a "neutral" sociologist.

At times I have tended to romanticize my fieldwork experience. That tendency helped sustain me from 1971 through 1974 and brought me back to 32nd Street in 1977 to find out what had happened to the youths I first met in 1971. Attending local dances, parties, weddings, and cotillions was exciting, and sitting on a park bench or walking around the neighborhood talking and observing was an adventure. Many families made me feel at home by inviting me to family functions and letting me know that I was always welcome. They celebrated my birthday and spent long hours making *tamales,* which they knew were among my favorite foods. The romantic adventure image helped me overcome my fears and bear the tedium of dictating notes at two or three in the morning, often six nights a week.

The adventure was often overshadowed by the fears and drudgery of doing fieldwork alone. Some of the problems I encountered were typical of all fieldwork, others stemmed from the nature of the community I had chosen. Entering an unknown setting with no set status or identity, introducing myself to many people, and remembering names and their pseudonyms used in my notes was not easy. In the beginning I regarded every resident as critical to my research and thought that offending any one of them would compel me to leave the field.

Though I was fluent in Spanish, life in Spain, Mexico, and North Philadelphia had not prepared me for doing research. After moving to 32nd Street in 1972, I quickly learned to distinguish between the sounds of gunfire and firecrackers and to block out the noise and music emanating from the pool hall below my apartment. However, I found the world of the streets sometimes a frightening place. Watching guns being passed through washroom windows to young women at public dances rattled me, particularly when we returned from the washroom to the dark, noisy dance floor, where a bystander could as easily have been shot as the intended victim.

Readers may wonder how a woman could possibly have spent time with gang members as they loitered on street corners and around park benches, and developed relationships that allowed her to gather sufficient and reliable data. I never tried to become a member of the community. The research role I developed through interaction with the youth varied from one group to another and was significantly influenced by some of my personal characteristics: I am Jewish, educated, small, fairly dark, a woman, dressed slightly sloppily but not *too* sloppily, and only a few years older than most of those whom I observed. These attributes did make a difference in how people appraised and evaluated me and my actions, and in the activities and thoughts to which I was privy. Careful observation of what kind of information was available to me and how different groups perceived and evaluated me allowed me to see not only what categories were important to each of the local groups and what someone in that role was permitted to see, do, and hear, but also how I should try to negotiate my identity in the field.

I had little choice but to acknowledge publicly the reasons for my presence on 32nd Street; not only do I differ in background from the 32nd Street residents but I had to violate many local expectations to gather the data I needed. While my appearance allowed me to blend into a youthful crowd, I sounded and looked sufficiently different so that most people realized immediately that I was not from the neighborhood. Much of the time it was advantageous to be an outsider and to be so regarded. For example, women do not spend time alone with male gangs as I did, especially without being affiliated with one of the gang's members. Moreover, as an outsider I could ask a lot of "stupid" questions— "Who are the guys in the black and red sweaters?" or "Why do you fight?" As anything but an acknowledged outsider I would have had a difficult time asking them.

While I spent some time with adults—teachers in several schools, families in their homes, and political activists in several community organizations—I spent most of my time with a variety of youth groups in the streets and at their other hangouts. Some of the youth were members of gangs who had and used guns; others were young women who frequently went out with these young men; others were much less involved in street life; and still others were college-bound.

Meeting young people was not as difficult as one might expect, given the public nature of much of their social life, particularly gang activity. In the first weeks of the project I chose to sit on a bench in a park where I saw many youth (aged 15 to 19) gathered from midafternoon until late at night. After several afternoons of sitting on a bench nearby, a male youth came over as I dropped a softball that had rolled toward me and said, "You can't catch" (which I acknowledged) and "You're not from the 'hood,' are you?" These were statements, not questions, by Gilberto, the Lions' president. I told him I wanted to write a book on Chicano youth. He told me that I should meet the "dudes" and took me over to shake hands with several of the members of the Lions gang. The park became my hangout every day after that, but it was several months, several bottles of Boone's Farm Strawberry Wine, and a number of rumors about my being a narcotics agent before many of the gang members would give me intimate information about their girlfriends, families, and feelings about themselves and the future. Some never did.

The facility with which I entered the community and eased into a fairly comfortable relationship with the Lions went to my head, and I nearly pushed my acceptance too far by not exercising a reasonable degree of caution. During my second month in the field, I heard about a gang peace meeting that was to take place on a Sunday afternoon at the park. All area gangs had been invited to attend. A perfect situation, I thought, a superb piece of data. On Sunday it was drizzling but I hurried down to 32nd Street. By 1:30 about 120 gang members had gathered under the porch of the park gym. Although I noticed that all the young women had disappeared from the park, I thought nothing of it.

The meeting began. A man in his late twenties started talking. I could not identify him as he was not wearing his "colors." He spoke for almost ten minutes about how the Chicano gangs had to stop fighting each other and instead get together for political purposes. Everyone listened attentively. Although I "saw" that several of them had guns, it did not register with me at the time.

Suddenly the speaker stopped and turned toward me, as did everyone else. My heart started doing triple time. He demanded, "Who are you?" I managed to say, "Hi! I'm Ruth and I'm writing a book on how the gangs are really together around here." Gilberto grabbed my arm, pulled me behind him, and said, "She's cool, she's been hanging with us." Another member of the Lions whispered to me to get out.

The gang member who challenged me at the peace conference was a Senior Greek. After the meeting I came back to the area where all the gangs were standing around. The speaker came toward me and invited me to join him and some other Senior Greeks at the corner tavern. They already had been drinking heavily. Frightened, but thinking only of the research opportunity, I followed them to the tavern. There they proceeded to tell me a story that sounded like the song "Officer Krupke" from *West Side Story:* They were "sick" and losers, the system was corrupt, and their parents had many problems. Over the next few years I got to know them much better, both how cruel and dangerous and how polite and thoughtful they could be.

My relationship with the male gang members evolved slowly and never was easy. Key elements of the identity we negotiated were my gender and the fact that I was an outsider. Being a woman both limited and expanded what I could see and do with the gang members. Remaining an outsider was essential. As a woman, I was not invited to attend fights or to go out looking for other gangs, but I was taken along to buy guns and was told afterwards about the fights, information that I would then verify with individual gang members and outside observers. I could talk to them about some aspects of their private lives, which they rarely discussed with other men. My lack of care with appearance, which both males and females continually remarked upon, allowed me to play down my sexual identity. However, I was very careful not to spend too much time alone with any one male and not to dance with them at the many parties and dances I attended.

The male gangs had a difficult time developing an identity for me that would allow them to be comfortable with a woman, as women do not hang around with men. However, as a woman I could do them little harm while they evaluated the situation; women can be harmful only when they are seen as controlling the situation. Gang members were the ones who could decide whether or not I could stay; I had made that option explicit. A man in a similar situation may have had a more difficult time, as his requests might be seen as a challenge. I later discovered that several weeks before I arrived a news photographer had had his camera taken from him and been told to leave.

The first dimension of my identity that I discovered they were constructing was as "a lady," which placed me in a respected but somewhat distant position from them. A "lady" implied that a woman was unobtainable sexually. One day when I was asked to accompany one of the members (age 15) to a corner grocery, we saw a young woman approaching and he said, "Here comes my girl." I had not met her and asked him if I should explain to her what I was doing. He replied that it was all right because she could see that I was a "lady." (His girl was not.) They began to treat me differently than the young women who sat in the park. They did not swear or discuss sex with a "lady," but did around some of the young women who spent time at the park. A man walked on the curb side with a "lady," helped to find her a chair, and took her arm to help her across an icy street; however, they did not do these things with most of the girls at the park. On several occasions a gang member would take my arm as we crossed an icy street, and when I dressed up for a fancy party, one of them rushed around to find me a comfortable chair. The youth frequently referred to their own mothers as "ladies." Here I was able to begin to discover the meaning of an important category to them and what they did in situations in which "ladies" are present.

However, "ladies" do not sit in the park and are not interested in gang members' lives. Social workers might be "ladies" who asked questions, but there were no outsider–social workers in the community, and the Lions discarded that category for me because I was at the park on evenings and weekends and did not try to make them do anything differently. Social workers worked from nine to five and told people what to do, they claimed. Finally, about four weeks after I arrived, and after examining the small notebook I carried with me, one of the gang members declared that I was like Lois Lane, the reporter (Superman's girlfriend). It was an identity that almost transcended gender. This provided them with the necessary identity with which I could ask about their activities and they could readily respond. Often they would seek me out to relay new stories of gang activities and, when someone wanted a story retold, to say, "Ask Ruth, she's been writing it all down."

Although the Lions began to treat me as a lady reporter, they still had misgivings as to what I was doing. Why would any outsider, particularly a woman, want to spend so much time with them? Both the researcher and the people who are being observed make sure the "data" are realistic by comparing them with their own ideas and experiences; the reliability of the data is checked by comparing what one is told with what is observed and with other accounts of the same events.

In the world of those whom I was observing, the police often asked questions. My behavior of asking questions and remaining in the background fit not only that of a reporter but also that of a "narc." A rumor that the narcotics squad was sending around a female agent gave rise to suspicion of my role. After I drank with them (fruit wines and beer) and watched them smoke marijuana and take acid without an arrest, that suspicion disappeared. Then they began to show me their weapons. One of the Lions showed me his radio, in which he had placed a small-caliber gun. He explained to me that he had seen guns put inside dictionaries on television, but he knew the police would be suspicious if they saw him carrying a book. When one of the Lions was arrested, not only did I make a small contribution to his bail but, as the only person over 21, I signed for him. Later I was asked and began to contribute small sums to the group's funds for beer and wine, which meant that they had decided that I was going to be around continuously. I had begun to notice that only those who were members of the group and always around contributed to the collective pot.

The outsider identity and somewhat marginal position of "lady reporter" allowed some closeness without being threatening as a woman who spent so much time with them asking what they often thought were dumb questions. This identity did not relegate me to lurking in the background, but allowed me to participate in many of the ongoing activities and was an indication of the limits of their interaction with adults in the wider society, their social skills, their categories of women, and the symbols they use to express the expected continuity of presence.

My identity as a lady reporter and the marginality that it implied had both advantages and disadvantages. Being a reporter allowed me to ask questions publicly about exciting events but not about family and personal experience. As a trusted, somewhat distant "lady," I had their respect. They would talk about their families in private; however, there were other things they would not discuss with or say in front of a "lady."

As a reporter I was allowed to check out accounts of fights by discussing them with individual members, the group, and older residents who had worked with gangs or had been members. From the very beginning, the gang members would talk about their fights and challenges by other gangs. Gathering data on fights and reputations was relatively easy, as it was seen that a reporter would be interested in their adventures.

Occasionally the subjects of school and work did arise naturally in the Lions' conversations; however, as a reporter and educated outsider I could probe these topics and probably extended them beyond their natural length in public discussions. School arose naturally as a topic of conversation when a particular event such as a fight, graduation, or suspension occurred. Work was a fairly common topic, as many of the Lions had worked, at least part time, from the age of 16. On other occasions, I would ask questions about school or work and, much of the time, a discussion would follow. As a recognized educated person (a reporter), I was asked questions about school and jobs.

Neither my identity as a reporter nor as a lady allowed me to obtain personal information concerning hopes, relationships with women, and families of the street youth. I was able to discover through conversations with former gang members that these were not topics discussed in public, and infrequently in private. Using the role of reporter was a failure; I tried to interview one of the gang members with a small portable tape recorder. He was so concerned about how he said things and "making a good story" that much of the material was so exaggerated and stilted that it was unusable. Only as a respected and trusted outsider was it possible for me to engage in such discussion.

The gang members could not discern what use personal information could be to me. However, they tried and failed to start rumors through me. In this way they gained confidence that I would not express their hopes and fears to others. They began to talk to me individually about themselves and the problems they had with their families and girlfriends.

Most of my discussions of family, girlfriends, and the future occurred when I would bump into one of the street-oriented males and he would ask for my advice about girlfriends, work, or school. Sometimes being slightly "high" encouraged the gang members to talk, but all questions had to be indirect. On one occasion I was talking to a Lion whose girl-friend had just told him that she was pregnant, when my reporter role got the best of me and I made the mistake of asking him why he had not used birth control in a tone that he took as an indictment of his behavior. With that comment, what had been a fascinating conversation about his intimate life, his fears of marriage and fatherhood, turned into a discus-sion of sports and fights. I had similar private conversations with many of the Lions and other street males, but some never felt close enough or trusted me enough to engage in such conversations.

On some occasions their evaluation of me as a "lady" proved an ad-vantage. It allowed me to remain uninvolved. Being a "lady" limited opportunities to attend gang fights; when several gang members would take off in a car to shoot at some "enemies" I was rarely invited. My refusal to go even when asked was readily honored. Additionally, when I was asked to hide a gun, being "a lady," not a reporter, gave me the needed excuse to refuse. Except for gang fights, they rarely told me about illegal activities before they occurred, although they usually in-formed me afterwards. In their view, reporters did not know about sto-ries until afterwards, and they were all aware that the wider society, of which I was a member, did not approve of much of their illegal behavior.

My identity as a "lady" did mean that swearing and public discus-sions of sexual exploits were limited. Watching how they reacted to me as a "lady," however, did tell me something about how they perceived that class of women. For example, one member was terribly embar-rassed when I picked up a book he was reading and discovered that it was a graphic account of someone's sexual exploits. "Ruth, you shouldn't see that kind of thing," he said as he grabbed the book back. Through other measures, I was able to find out that they often discussed sex. When a male friend who was researching "rich kids" (which they found amusing) joined me at the park, they told him that they never talked about sex in front of me. There was no identity I could negotiate that would allow me to be privy to discussions of sex. I was unable to explore how they used public discussions of sexual relations and, therefore, was unable to explore the meaning of such discussions to group status and relationships.

*   *   *

Identities are not fixed, but are affirmed or changed continually. It was an advantage to be appraised as a lady and a reporter, as that identity allowed me to maintain a degree of distance and legitimacy as a woman among men. However, the longer I remained with the group, the more I became aware that some of the young men were attempting to redefine my identity as a potential girlfriend, making my sexual identity salient. After more than a year of using "lady reporter" as a key identity, some members began to flirt seriously and tried to ask me out. They claimed that my age (six to eight years older) did not constitute a barrier to starting a relationship. They were trying to replace my identity as a lady reporter with an identity that encompassed my potential as a sexual partner, regardless of my efforts to deemphasize my appearance and emphasize our age difference and my outsider status.

My failure to dress well initially acted as a deterrent to their appraising me in terms of my sexual identity. In contrast to my unpressed (but clean and unpatched) jeans, T-shirts or turtlenecks, and flat rubber-soled shoes or sandals, and my lack of make-up or a sophisticated hairstyle, the majority of young women on 32nd Street were much more concerned with appearance and dressed more neatly and fashionably in the latest style jeans or slacks (always well pressed), pretty blouses, and make-up. My lack of what they considered decent clothing and my inability to do anything with my hair were frequently a source of comment. One of the gang members teased me for two days when he noticed (immediately) that I had bought a new pair of shoes to replace the ones with holes, and several of the young women offered to lend me outfits when we discussed an upcoming dance. The young women frequently worried about my ability to "catch a man." While I dressed within the acceptable range, the remarks concerning my inability to dress well led me to see how important appearance was for both men and women. They also served, at first, to downplay my role as a sexual object.

Several of my actions may have encouraged the gang members' attempts to renegotiate my identity as an insider and sexual object. My move into a small apartment in the community was interpreted as a possible indication of community membership. Moreover, a friend from out of town came to visit, making the Lions aware that I might be attracted to some men, so they could begin to ask, "Why not us?" I had provided them with new information that they could interpret as indicating a need to change my identity.

While I was continually at the point of losing my lady reporter identity, I was not challenged all the time. I remained wary, making sure that other women were included on trips to the Lions' clubhouse and not dancing at parties. However, the attempts to renegotiate my identity began to limit my mobility and discussions with the gang and to reemphasize the importance of the wide gap between acceptable male and female roles and "ladies" and "chicks" that I had been observing.

As a lady reporter marginal to the community, I did not have to be treated as a sexual object and was free to spend time with men and ask questions. However, as an independent person I did not appear to be subordinate, which was threatening to their views of themselves as men who dominated women. Not only did I come and go as I wished, but I knew a lot about them. From their perspective, that gave me control. After fifteen months, their sexual teasing increased significantly; they commented about how good I looked, asked if I would go out with them, and several stated that I knew too much about them.

I did not know much more about their fighting, number of guns, or other illegal activities than many community residents. That was not what they were worried about. Rather, I knew too much about them as people—their problems, weaknesses, hopes, and fears. They needed one another and they knew that I knew that. I knew them too well and was aware that they were not all that they publicly claimed to be (tough warriors). They masked their intimacy and need for one another in order to be perceived publicly as tough. As soon as they began to see me as a potential sexual partner, my independence and possible control over them through intimate knowledge became problematic for them. As a woman, I should have been subordinate, but I was dominant through my independence and had potential power over them based on my intimate knowledge about them.

A sexual identity would have greatly impeded the research process. This culture creates strong parameters within which a female researcher would be very constrained as a community member. As the pressures increased to take a locally defined membership role, I was unable to negotiate a gender identity that would allow me to continue as a researcher. After eighteen months I had to stop spending so much time with the gangs and turned to the study of other youth groups in the community, seeing the gang members on occasion.

Douglas Harper

Relations of the Road

Douglas Harper has spent years studying the lives of people on urban skid rows and in hobo jungles. In his book Good Company *he discusses his experiences as a participant observer in the hobo's world. He contrasts the life of tramps who ride freight trains and find casual labor in the cities and western fruit farms with the more sedentary, yet also more self-destructive, life of skid-row bums.*

Photographs were an important part of the material Harper collected while living with the tramps. They became "a visual inventory of typical behavior in typical spaces—for this group." But as the following account illustrates, the photos could not be allowed to intrude on his participation in the tramp life.

Also important to Harper's research was his friendship with a long-time tramp, Carl, who became his companion on the journey described in Good Company. *Carl educated the sociologist-photographer, explaining how to survive on the road, showing him how to interact with other tramps, and eventually telling him his own story. In fact, the growing friendship between Harper and Carl was typical of how tramps come together on the road, share each other's lives for a time, and then part company.*

Of course, in order to conduct his research Harper had to learn how

This selection is adapted from Douglas Harper, *Good Company.* © 1982 by The University of Chicago. Abridgment © 1989 by The University of Chicago. All rights reserved. Adapted with permission of The University of Chicago Press.

*to locate trains and board them without being driven out of the yards.
Freight trains are dangerous and difficult to ride, and riding them is
illegal. Mastering the trains requires resourcefulness, cunning, persis-
tence, and intelligence. For the tramp, the trains are a proving ground.
For Harper, too, there was a process of initiation, a period in which he
felt too intimidated to ride the trains, and eventually a feeling of confidence and even pleasure as he grew to understand the hobo's life. An
especially striking aspect of this selection is the mixture of fear and joy
he experienced as he climbed onto a train and reentered the tramp world.*

I'd been waiting for a train a year before in the same yard heading in
the same direction but nothing seemed particularly familiar. The Minneapolis Burlington Northern yards stretch northwest from under the
University and they go on for miles; ten, fifteen, twenty tracks wide;
spurs heading north, spurs heading east; and somewhere in the maze a
main line that carries the hotshot out of Chicago through Minneapolis to
the west. I stood in the shadows of huge grain elevators, out of sight of
the control tower, and I waited for a train due at midnight.

I'd been in the yards a couple of days, peeking around, asking questions and making plans. Every time I've come back to the freights I've
had to cross an emotional hurdle—they seem too big, too fast, too dangerous, and too illegal—and I get used to the idea by spending a few
days in the yards, testing the waters. If the brakemen aren't busy they'll
answer a carefully worded question. If there are railroad police around
it's better to encounter them just hanging around; no gear and no suspicious behavior. Then you choose the day: Tomorrow you'll ride; tonight
you'll party and pack your gear and tomorrow you'll be back on the
road. Then when you walk past the No Trespassing signs into the yard
your traveling clothes and your gear mark you clearly. You enter a world
that has its own rules and few second chances, and you'd better know
what you're up to.

I was shifting back into a tramp world for the fourth or fifth time. I'd
made cross-country trips on freights and I'd spent some weeks the winter before living on Boston's skid row. While my purpose was to describe a tramp way of life, it was only part of the reason I'd go back
again and again. The taste of camp coffee and the view from a flatcar on
a slow ride through the Rockies were magnets that pulled hard indeed.
This time I felt my gear in order and plans set. The Chicago hotshot
would carry me across the Dakotas, Montana, and the Rockies. As much
as I had a destination it was Wenatchee, Washington, for I knew it to
be the center of the apple country and a junction of major rail lines. I
knew the jungles in Wenatchee and I knew that there would be tramps
there to steer me to a job. The Chicago hotshot, with the right connec-

tions, should get me to Wenatchee in no more than a couple of days. I mulled it over and relaxed. It seemed manageable, and it seemed in grasp.

After perhaps half an hour the activity increased in the yard. Strings of boxcars were pushed up and down the parallel tracks, shuffled into boxcars, flatcars, gondolas, and piggybacks that were then pushed uncoupled over the hump. The humped cars slammed into pieces of trains down one of the fifteen or twenty tracks that led away from the small hill. It was all controlled by invisible workers in a control tower that loomed above. The cars were shuffled and reshuffled; a few empties or badorders set off and pushed aside; a string of piggybacks or gondolas pushed into place—it went on and on like a carefully rehearsed play. I watched idly until I noticed a long string of empty grain cars and flatcars moving into place. I guessed that the grain cars would be going west, probably to Minot or Havre, and that the flats would go on to the lumbering country in the Rockies. As the train stretched out further and further I decided to find out.

I picked my way across the yard. It is with utmost care that one climbs over the couplings of boxcars for it is impossible to know when a car or engine will slam into it, compressing the long shaft on which the coupling is mounted and setting the car into a slow roll. The proper procedure is to throw one's gear over the couplings, then to climb across the space on the ladders and the braces on the car itself. It is quickly apparent in a freight yard that the scale is unhuman—a small jolt to a freight car or a small compression of a coupling is enough to fling a person from the car and if you fall off climbing over you'll be run over or dragged down the yard. I moved over the couplings, first with hesitancy and then with more confidence as I found my "rail legs."

I found the longest section of train and began walking its length. I walked down the narrow canyon between the cars and came upon a tramp crouched near the door of the first empty boxcar. He did not see me coming and displeasure crossed his face when I suddenly appeared. He smelled of booze, sweat, and urine and his work uniform looked like he'd slept in it for a week. His face was scarred and unshaven. He had some gear back in the boxcar; I asked him where he was headed. It was clear he wanted nothing to do with me but he answered that he was going west to pick apples. I told him that I too was going to Wenatchee to pick apples, but he answered, not a little sarcastically, that there wasn't any good work in *Wenatchee*, you had to go north, up the Okanagan to a place like Oroville. Before I could ask him where that was he'd slunk back to the corner of his car. I walked on to find my own.

I was nearly to the end of the train before I found another empty boxcar. It was old and battered, without wooden liners on the walls that would cool and quiet the ride. The wheels were mounted in old-style bearings that make an empty car jump and skitter, and the floor was covered with strapping iron and sawdust. I did not like the car but it was the only inside ride on the train. I checked to see if it was a badorder on its way to a repair yard before I threw my gear in the door.

I found some cardboard sheets to make a mattress and pushed some of the litter out of the car. A brakeman stuck his head in the door and startled me with a greeting. He told me the train was due out on the highline—the old Great Northern tracks—as soon as it got its power. It would make the 500-mile run to Minot before breaking up and it should get me there a few hours before the hotshot which was due at midnight, so I'd be able to catch a few hours sleep before continuing on. Then our conversation should have been over but he lingered. He told me he'd tramped all over the west when he was younger and he always tried to help a man out "as long as they looked like they knew what they were doing." It was all going down hill, he said; the tramps were bums and there were hippies on the trains always getting into trouble. You don't mind a rider, he repeated, if they know what they're doing. But the hippie will lie around in the open smoking dope as though it's a picnic, and then they'll get hurt and sue the railroad. He shook his head to show his disgust, and walked away.

As the engine jockied into position at the front of the train my car was slammed backward and forward. I worked quickly to peg the doors open with old brake linings and railroad spikes I found lying around the yard. It is an important job, for if the doors jolt shut there is no way to open them from the inside. As I worked, a yard engine lumbered by, sounding like it was overrevving with the pent-up power of huge diesel engines pushing it oh so slowly by. Two green Burlington Northern engines, attached back to back, idled alongside and past my boxcar. I caught sight of the engineer and our eyes met briefly but his expression did not change. Just a minute later the air hissed down the brakelines and the highball whistle blew. I was filled with a lonely sort of expectancy—an intense desire to be under way. Then the engineer snapped the throttle back, the jolt crashed down the train and the trip began.

As the train gained speed the memories came flooding back. The noise and movement are soon more than I've experienced. Nothing can be so loud! Nothing can throw me about with such abandon! The car, sprung for hundreds of tons, carries me as a tiny piece of flotsam bouncing, banging, swaying. The car rocks from side to side and I think of empty boxcars tipping and taking whole freight trains with them. You don't live through those, say the tramps. The car bangs so hard on road crossings I hold my mouth open to keep my teeth from cracking together. I try to sit and my body leaps off the floor and my sleeping bag skitters away. Slack creeps into the mile-long train and as the car suddenly snaps ahead I find my body accomplishing the anatomical feat of moving three directions at once. I stand with my legs spread for balance, holding a wall to keep from pitching over, bending my knees to take up the shock of the ride. The train highballs and the tracks are bad and my car rides worse than any I remember. Or perhaps it just seems this way every time I go back. The eight hours ahead seem interminable but the train does not slow to ease my aches.

I spend the hours standing by the doors. When the tracks parallel a highway I catch a glimpse of car travelers safely encapsulated. Sometimes they wave but more often they look away and shield their children from the sight of me. An outlaw so soon! I laugh aloud but I cannot hear myself above the din of the train. I am captured by the absurdity. I run back and forth through the car; leap, play, dash about. The train moves on its own; I'm but a small grain attached. With all the swirling grit my trip is cleaner by far than those on the highway for there is no windshield constricting my view and no billboard to funnel my attention. I feel the land, standing quite near, and it becomes very much a part of my trip.

I pass through time as the train slices through pink and avocado subdivisions of towns; through belts of older, taller, and more muted houses; and finally through stone-facaded mainstreets. The train depots had been the kernels from which these towns grew, but now only an old trainman stands on the platform and waves as the freight highballs through.

We pass for an hour through an area dotted with lakes before entering the Red River valley. The transformation is quick and complete. Fields of sunflowers stretch to the horizon; then come quarter section after quarter section of corn with farm buildings and houses tucked into small tree-filled corners and straight and regular roads tying it all together.

Well into the evening the train slowed for the first time to a 15-mile-an-hour idle through the Fargo/Moorhead yards and I watched ten or twelve tramps waiting to board. I stood in the door to claim my space and they stayed away from my car. I was glad to be left alone when the train pulled into the North Dakota prairie.

As the sun set, the train turned due west. I looked around the edge of the door and watched the mile-long train bore directly into the orange sun on the horizon. It got dark fast and I became depressed, feeling quite alone. I was nearly overcome with tiredness before I crawled into my sleeping bag and fought my way to sleep in the lurching, rocking, and screeching freight car.

*   *   *

The next days brought a slow ride on bull locals through the Dakotas, Montana, Idaho, and Wahsington. I'd missed a connection or the brakeman had lied to me, but either way I was far from the fast trains of the highline. The tramp I'd met in Minneapolis, sour from his three-week drunk, broke and hungry, had become my companion. I had a loaf of bread made into peanut butter and jelly sandwiches, and even though it became a sticky oozing mess in the heat of a Montana August, it kept us going for a couple of days. The tramp made it clear that he would have preferred beans. As he sobered up, our relationship quietly began.

"You know," he said once after we had been together for a couple of days, "you can't trust everybody you meet. I can see it in your manner. You're too open, you're—what's the word—too naive."

"That may be, but you left your gear with me plenty of times. I could've taken off with it."

"You aren't goin' nowhere. Got too much shit of your own. Anyway, you don't know enough to be afraid of. This life ain't no bed of roses. I've lost too much gear not to know that. You know how much this sleeping bag cost me? That's forty-five dollars right there. It's what they call a Red Fox. It's got that new-fangled material in it."

"It's good to travel with a sleeping bag," I said.

"Yeah, *if* you can keep it. You know the people you work with, they're bigger thieves than anybody. And then there are guys just to rob you, to git your money and your gear."

"Are these regular tramps you're talking about?"

"Well, they travel the country like your regular tramps, but they ain't no tramps. We call them jackrollers. And once in a while you'll get young kids that'll do the same thing. You can't trust anybody, and I ain't kidding. Where we're headed, up there north of Wenatchee, that's country you got to be careful of. Ain't too bad goin' in, but comin' out, after the harvest, then you got to be careful. What I always do is make my wages and ride out of there payin'. Let that freight go all alone. And I seldom drink on the freight—I'll take it somewhere else.

"You got to understand something—you're just a tramp, and nobody wants nothun' to do with you unless it's your money or your work. The cops are no different. I got busted for drunk in Spokane last year, hell, I hadn't seen a bottle for three days! An' you always leave jail with clean pockets. But the worst ones are the jackrollers. See this one?" The tramp pointed to a scar that led from the corner of his left eye down along his nose and across his lips. "That happened in Minneapolis. All they got off me that time was four dollars in cash and ten dollars' worth of groceries."

"Were you drunk?"

"Hell, no, I was asleep. Woke up in the Hennepin County Hospital; they hit me in the face. Just missed my eye."

"Where were you staying?"

"I was *heading* west."

"Were you in a freight yard? In a boxcar?"

"Hell, no, I was out in the weeds. It's easy to find a man in a boxcar. You're a sitting duck in a boxcar. But they follow you out to the weeds, too. They watch, they watch for you and follow you out. *You'll* get it if you're not careful. I won't lay down in that boxcar, either, unless it's moving. And when that train is moving I got one eye open and I'm on my feet the moment he stops . . .

"You'll see, it's all changing. Used to be all you'd find on this road was the tramp, and this time of year it would be the fruit tramp, what we call the apple knocker. But nowadays they're not all tramps. Seattle is so damn screwed up they'll come out of there to find work. And they're starting to get Mexicans in some places. Your real tramps won't associate with them. But most of the Mexicans stay down south, thinnin' beets, that's good work for them. Stoop labor, that's what they like. And the government's gettin' on a lot of camps where you'd live, closing them up. They're filthy places. But then there is no place for a man to stay. You have to carry a tent. I know some guys that do it, carry a tent. Lightweight tents. And sometimes you'll build a shack. One guy will work days, the other nights. That way there'll always be somebody around to watch the stuff. But you got to be careful, really careful. I camped with a man and a woman last year and they stole what I had. Panasonic radio, worth forty dollars. AM/FM radio. Twelve bucks' worth of groceries. And my bag with my change of clothes in it. But I know who they are and sooner or later I'll get them. You can't escape on this road—everybody knows you after a while . . ."

The tramp and I spent a month together, winding our way across the west to the apple harvest in northern Washington State. We jungled together with other tramps in the harvest town and were eventually hired out to pick apples. We met a tramp he'd known for years and he taught me the proper tramp etiquette. We'd "buddied-up," as tramps typically do—by sharing food, supplies, time, and miles—but Carl taught me that a tramp makes his own decisions and eventually moves on alone. He accepted my food because he was down and out, but he knew I was not a regular and he was suspicious of what he'd have to pay. During our first days together he realized I did not really know what to expect from him and he warned: "Some people on this road are helpless. When you start helpin' it's just like having a son . . . They don't know where it stops! You got to support them—take care of them—you got to provide the hand and I won't do that. If a fella is on this road and he can't learn—then to hell with him." Later he added: "When you get your job, don't depend on nobody else. If you want to leave, then leave! That's it—a lot of these guys say, 'If you quit, let me know and I'll quit with you.' I say bullshit. Before you know it you'll have run out of places to work."

I understood even less, I realized very early, about relationships I observed among other tramps. As I watched an elaborate exchange of coffee, food, and clothes between Blackie and Carl I noted what I thought to be a wonderful generosity that existed on the road. Later I learned that Blackie was a sonofabitch trying to get Carl indebted for future business. Yet later when we jungled before the harvest there were few supplies anywhere and everything a tramp had became common property. I slowly and awkwardly came to understand these events and to participate in them in a way that could be called normal by those in the life.

But even though Carl tried to make our relationship typical, it never was. At first he taught me how to make it on the road and ignored most of my questions. Something changed the chemistry between us and he stepped out of his normal role to tell me about his childhood, his parents, and his life before hitting the road. I had learned not to expect such self-revelations, and I think Carl sensed as well that they constituted transgressions of the normal tramp way. At the end he distanced himself again and made it clear that the things we had been discussing were off limits and that when it came time to leave he would be on his way alone.

My sociological eye observed all this, yet my emotional character acted on its own. In becoming committed to Carl the individual (as opposed to Carl the tramp) I offered unwanted advice and rather unconsciously set out to reform my buddy. Carl humored me—I told him he ought to put a part of his stash in the bank before he started a binge, and he said: "I do—bartender's bank!" Or, just after telling me he expected to buy a cabin in Montana and I said I'd like that too, he replied: "That's what I want to get away from . . . neighbors." But finally, I began to feel a grudging respect and a partial acceptance. Just before I left he said: "I've noticed you change. You've learned that you can make it on the road—now if something overloads it'll always be in the back of your mind. You watch yourself—you'll be reverting back."

But as I became more like Carl in manner and behavior, and perhaps more hardened by the experiences we shared, I could not leave my other values behind. When he opened up to me I responded with friendship (a category from my life, not his). When he distanced himself I felt rebuffed, and I felt a great loss at the end of our time together. I never really learned to experience the world as a tramp and I knew that unless I moved completely into that life my values would probably remain in the world of relationships and commitments.

*   *   *

As I involved myself more I had to reassess my purpose and methods. I could have continued as I had begun and produced a photographic study from the viewpoint of an outsider, but as I felt myself pulled into the life, my photographic activity changed very much. On the trip I have described I carried a Leica and a single lens—a small, unobtrusive and quiet camera. I made few photographs during my time with Carl. I introduced myself as a writer and photographer and he did not seem to mind my taking pictures until we encountered people he'd known for a long time; then he made it clear that to carry on would be out of the question. Some of the photographs I did make, however, show how the camera may describe the relation between "researcher" and "informant." The image that communicates this best is of Carl handing me a piece of toast. The toast was made at my request. The fire was the first we'd made in days. A long trip was nearly completed and our relationship had the quality of those in which important events have been shared. I am satisfied with the photograph for it describes both an important activity and the nature of our relationship. The photographs I did not take, of Boston Blackie, One-Eyed Jack, and the jungles along the way testify by their absence to the same issue. The relationship between the photographer and subject in a fieldwork experience is very complicated, but for me the rights and desires of the individuals we choose as subjects are more important than a final purpose that would justify making images when they would not be welcomed. The camera must sometimes be left behind.

Photo courtesy of Douglas Harper.

Photo courtesy of Douglas Harper.

Photo courtesy of Douglas Harper.

Part III

Maintaining Objectivity

My work would have to be a full-length portrait, light and darkness with more shading than sharp lines. Since neutrality was impossible and idealization undesirable, I settled on striving for balance. If these people emerged as real in their entire human range and variety, arousing admiration and disappointment, laughter and tears, hope and despair, I would be satisfied.

Barbara Myerhoff

William F. Whyte

Doing Research in Cornerville

William Foote Whyte's study of life in an Italian-American slum has become a classic of the sociological literature. Whyte conducted his research in "Cornerville," a slum district of a large East Coast city, for three and a half years. During much of that time he lived with an Italian family, not only to obtain an intimate view of family life but also to establish contacts with the wider community. He learned Italian, joined in community activities such as bowling and baseball, and gained the confidence and friendship of the residents of Cornerville.

Whyte's analysis of Cornerville focused on the structure and leadership of informal groups of "corner boys" and their relations with other groups within the community, especially political organizations, racketeering organizations, and the police. The results of his research were published in his famous book Street Corner Society.

In this selection Whyte describes how he obtained a sponsor, Doc, who introduced him to all the individuals and groups he wished to study. As Whyte puts it, this situation was "perfect." Despite his good fortune in meeting Doc, however, Whyte encountered a number of obstacles in the course of his research. In discussing his experiences he points out that "the researcher, like his informants, is a social animal." If re-

This selection is adapted from William F. Whyte, *Street Corner Society: The Social Structure of an Italian Slum.* © 1943, 1955, 1981 by The University of Chicago. Abridgment © 1989 by The University of Chicago. All rights reserved. Adapted with permission of The University of Chicago Press.

searchers live for an extended period in the community they are study-
ing, their personal life is inextricably mixed with their research. Each
researcher deals with this issue somewhat differently, but each must deal
with it in some way.

In the following pages Whyte describes how he merged his personal
life with that of his friends and neighbors, but in this introduction it is
worth mentioning that his integration into the life of the community had
some intriguing consequences. In the fall of 1937 the position of mayor
of Eastern City was up for election. Whyte joined the campaign of one
of the candidates, running errands and doing odd jobs such as nailing
up posters in various parts of the district. On election day he voted and
then reported for duty at the campaign headquarters. As the voting pro-
ceeded, it became evident that the opposition candidate was stealing the
election. The solution: All the supporters of Whyte's candidate were to
go out and vote again—several times.

Eventually Whyte learned that to be accepted by the people in a com-
munity it is not necessary to do everything just the way they do it. But
as is true for many researchers in the field, it was a lesson learned the
hard way.

When I began my work, I had had no training in sociology or anthropology. At the time I was sitting in on a course in slums and housing in the
Sociology Department at Harvard. As a term project I took on a study
of one block in Cornerville. To legitimize this effort, I got in touch with
a private agency that concerned itself in housing matters and offered to
turn over to them the results of my survey. With that backing, I began
knocking on doors, looking into flats, and talking to the tenants about
the living conditions. This brought me into contact with Cornerville people, but it would be hard now to devise a more inappropriate way of
beginning a study such as I was eventually to make.

Shortly thereafter I met a young economics instructor at Harvard who
impressed me with his self-assurance and his knowledge of Eastern City.
He had once been attached to a settlement house, and he talked glibly
about his associations with the tough young men and women of the district. He also described how he would occasionally drop in on some
drinking place in the area and strike up an acquaintance with a girl, buy
her a drink, and then encourage her to tell him her life-story. He claimed
that the women so encountered were appreciative of this opportunity
and that it involved no further obligation.

This approach seemed at least as plausible as anything I had been able
to think of. I resolved to try it out. I picked on the Regal Hotel, which
was on the edge of Cornerville. With some trepidation I climbed the
stairs to the bar and entertainment area and looked around. There I en-

countered a situation for which my adviser had not prepared me. There were women present all right, but none of them was alone. Some were there in couples, and there were two or three pairs of women together. I pondered this situation briefly. I had little confidence in my skill at picking up one female, and it seemed inadvisable to tackle two at the same time. Still, I was determined not to admit defeat without a struggle. I looked around me again and now noticed a threesome: one man and two women. It occurred to me that here was a maldistribution of females which I might be able to rectify. I approached the group and opened with something like this: "Pardon me. Would you mind if I joined you?" There was a moment of silence while the man stared at me. He then offered to throw me downstairs. I assured him that this would not be necessary and demonstrated as much by walking right out of there without any assistance.

For my next effort I sought out the local settlement houses. They were open to the public. You could walk right into them, and—though I would not have phrased it this way at the time—they were manned by middle-class people like myself. I realized even then that to study Cornerville I would have to go well beyond the settlement house, but perhaps the social workers could help me to get started.

It was at the settlement house that I met Doc. I had talked to a number of the social workers about my plans and hopes to get acquainted with the people and study the district. They listened with varying degrees of interest. If they had suggestions to make, I have forgotten them now except for one. Somehow, in spite of the vagueness of my own explanations, the head of girls' work in the Norton Street House understood what I needed. She began describing Doc to me. He was, she said, a very intelligent and talented person who had at one time been fairly active in the house but had dropped out, so that he hardly ever came in any more. Perhaps he could understand what I wanted, and he must have the contacts that I needed. She said she frequently encountered him as she walked to and from the house and sometimes stopped to chat with him. If I wished, she would make an appointment for me to see him in the house one evening. This at last seemed right. I jumped at the chance. As I came into the district that evening, it was with a feeling that here I had my big chance to get started. Somehow Doc must accept me and be willing to work with me.

The social worker showed us into her office and then left so that we could talk. Doc waited quietly for me to begin, as he sank down into a chair. I found him a man of medium height and spare build. His hair was a light brown, quite a contrast to the more typical black Italian hair. It was thinning around the temples. His cheeks were sunken. His eyes were a light blue and seemed to have a penetrating gaze.

I began by asking him if the social worker had told him about what I was trying to do.

"No, she just told me that you wanted to meet me and that I should like to meet you."

Then I went into a long explanation. I said that I had been interested in congested city districts in my college study but had felt very remote from them. I hoped to study the problems in such a district. I felt I could do very little as an outsider. Only if I could get to know the people and learn their problems first hand would I be able to gain the understanding I needed.

Doc heard me out without any change of expression, so that I had no way of predicting his reaction. When I was finished, he asked: "Do you want to see the high life or the low life?"

"I want to see all that I can. I want to get as complete a picture of the community as possible."

"Well, any nights you want to see anything, I'll take you around. I can take you to the joints—gambling joints—I can take you around to the street corners. Just remember that you're my friend. That's all they need to know. I know these places, and, if I tell them that you're my friend, nobody will bother you. You just tell me what you want to see, and we'll arrange it."

The proposal was so perfect that I was at a loss for a moment as to how to respond to it. We talked a while longer, as I sought to get some pointers as to how I should behave in his company. He warned me that I might have to take the risk of getting arrested in a raid on a gambling joint but added that this was not serious. I only had to give a false name and then would get bailed out by the man that ran the place, paying only a five-dollar fine. I agreed to take this chance. I asked him whether I should gamble with others in the gambling joints. He said it was unnecessary and, for a greenhorn like myself, very inadvisable.

At last I was able to express my appreciation. "You know, the first steps of getting to know a community are the hardest. I could see things going with you that I wouldn't see for years otherwise."

"That's right. You tell me what you want to see, and we'll arrange it. When you want some information, I'll ask for it, and you listen. When you want to find out their philosophy of life, I'll start an argument and get it for you. If there's something else you want to get, I'll stage an act for you. Not a scrap, you know, but just tell me what you want, and I'll get it for you."

"That's swell. I couldn't ask for anything better. Now I'm going to try to fit in all right, but, if at any time you see I'm getting off on the wrong foot, I want you to tell me about it."

"Now we're being too dramatic. You won't have any trouble. You come in as my friend. When you come in like that, at first everybody will treat you with respect. You can take a lot of liberties, and nobody will kick. After a while when they get to know you they will treat you like anybody else—you know, they say familiarity breeds contempt. But you'll never have any trouble. There's just one thing to watch out for. Don't spring [treat] people. Don't be too free with your money.''

"You mean they'll think I'm a sucker?"

"Yes, and you don't want to buy your way in."

That was our beginning. At the time I found it hard to believe that I could move in as easily as Doc had said with his sponsorship. But that indeed was the way it turned out.

While I was taking my first steps with Doc, I was also finding a place to live in Cornerville. To meet people, to get to know them, to fit into their activities, required spending time with them—a lot of time day after day. Commuting to Cornerville, you might come in on a particular afternoon and evening only to discover that the people you intended to see did not happen to be around at the time. Or, even if you did see them, you might find the time passing entirely uneventfully. You might just be standing around with people whose only occupation was talking or walking about to try to keep themselves from being bored. Only if I lived in Cornerville would I ever be able to understand it and be accepted by it. Finding a place, however, was not easy. In such an overcrowded district a spare room was practically nonexistent. I might have been able to take a room in the Norton Street Settlement House, but I realized that I must do better than this if possible.

I got my best lead from the editor of a weekly English-language newspaper published for the Italian-American colony. I had talked to him before about my study and had found him sympathetic. Now I came to ask him for help in finding a room. He directed me to the Martinis, a family which operated a small restaurant. I went there for lunch and later consulted the son of the family. He was sympathetic but said that they had no place for any additional person. Still, I liked the place and enjoyed the food. I came back several times just to eat. On one occasion I met the editor, and he invited me to his table. We discussed my rooming problem again. I mentioned the possibility of living at the Norton Street House. He nodded but added: "It would be much better if you could be in a family. You would pick up the language much quicker, and you would get to know the people. But you want a nice family, an educated family. You don't want to get in with any low types. You want a real good family."

At this he turned to the son of the family with whom I had spoken and asked: "Can't you make some place for Mr. Whyte in the house here?"

Al Martini paused a moment and then said: "Maybe we can fix it up. I'll talk to Mama again."

So he did talk to Mama again, and they did find a place. In fact, he turned over to me his own room and moved in to share a double bed with the son of the cook. I protested mildly at this imposition, but everything had been decided—except for the money. They did not know what to charge me, and I did not know what to offer. Finally, after some fencing, I offered fifteen dollars a month, and they settled for twelve.

Physically, the place was livable, and it provided me with more than just a physical base. I had been with the Martinis for only a week when I discovered that I was much more than a roomer to them. I had been taking many of my meals in the restaurant and sometimes stopping in to chat with the family before I went to bed at night. Then one afternoon I was out at Harvard and found myself coming down with a bad cold. Since I still had my Harvard room, it seemed the sensible thing to do to stay overnight there. I did not think to tell the Martinis of my plan.

The next day when I was back in the restaurant for lunch, Al Martini greeted me warmly and then said that they had all been worried when I did not come home the night before. Mama had stayed up until two o'clock waiting for me. As I was just a young stranger in the city, she could visualize all sorts of things happening to me. Al told me that Mama had come to look upon me as one of the family. I was free to come and go as I pleased, but she wouldn't worry so much if she knew of my plans.

I was very touched by this plea and resolved thereafter to be as good a son as I could to the Martinis.

At first I communicated with Mama and Papa primarily in smiles and gestures. Papa knew no English at all, and Mama's knowledge was limited to one sentence which she would use when some of the young boys on the street were making noise below her window when she was trying to get her afternoon nap. She would then poke her head out of the window and shout: "Goddam-sonumabitcha! Geroutahere!"

Some weeks earlier, in anticipation of moving into the district, I had begun working on the Italian language myself with the aid of a Linguaphone. One morning now Papa Martini came by when I was talking to the phonograph record. He listened for a few moments in the hall trying to make sense out of this peculiar conversation. Then he burst in on me with fascinated exclamations. We sat down together while I demonstrated the machine and the method to him. After that he delighted in working with me, and I called him my language professor. In a short time we reached a stage where I could carry on simple conversations, and, thanks to the Linguaphone and Papa Martini, the Italian that came out apparently sounded authentic. He liked to try to pass me off to his friends as *paesano mio*—a man from his own home town in Italy.

Since my research developed so that I was concentrating almost exclusively upon the younger, English-speaking generation, my knowledge of Italian proved unnecessary for research purposes. Nevertheless, I feel certain that it was important in establishing my social position in Cornerville—even with that younger generation. There were schoolteachers and social workers who had worked in Cornerville for as much as twenty years and yet had made no effort to learn Italian. My effort to learn the language probably did more to establish the sincerity of my interest in the people than anything I could have told them of myself and my work.

My days with the Martinis would pass in this manner. I would get up in the morning around nine o'clock and go out to breakfast. Al Martini told me I could have breakfast in the restaurant, but, for all my desire to fit in, I never could take their breakfast of coffee with milk and a crust of bread.

After breakfast, I returned to my room and spent the rest of the morning, or most of it, typing up my notes regarding the previous day's events. I had lunch in the restaurant and then set out for the street corner. Usually I was back for dinner in the restaurant and then out again for the evening.

Usually I came home again between eleven and twelve o'clock, at a time when the restaurant was empty except perhaps for a few family friends. Then I might join Papa in the kitchen to talk as I helped him dry the dishes, or pull up a chair into a family conversation around one of the tables next to the kitchen. There I had a glass of wine to sip, and I could sit back and mostly listen but occasionally try out my growing Italian on them.

Though I made several useful contacts in the restaurant or through the family, it was not for this that the Martinis were important to me. There is a strain to doing such fieldwork. The strain is greatest when you are a stranger and are constantly wondering whether people are going to accept you. But, much as you enjoy your work, as long as you are observing and interviewing, you have a role to play, and you are not completely relaxed. It was a wonderful feeling at the end of a day's work to be able to come home to relax and enjoy myself with the family. Probably it would have been impossible for me to carry on such a concentrated study of Cornerville if I had not had such a home from which to go out and to which I might return.

*   *   *

I can still remember my first outing with Doc. We met one evening at the Norton Street House and set out from there to a gambling place a couple of blocks away. I followed Doc anxiously down the long, dark hallway at the back of a tenement building. I was not worried about the possibility of a police raid. I was thinking about how I would fit in and be accepted. The door opened into a small kitchen almost bare of furnishings and with the paint peeling off the walls. As soon as we went in the door, I took off my hat and began looking around for a place to hang it. There was no place. I looked around, and here I learned my first lesson in participant observation in Cornerville: Don't take off your hat in the house—at least not when you are among men. It may be permissible, but certainly not required, to take your hat off when women are around.

Doc introduced me as "my friend Bill" to Chichi, who ran the place, and to Chichi's friends and customers. I stayed there with Doc part of the time in the kitchen, where several men would sit around and talk, and part of the time in the other room watching the crap game.

There was talk about gambling, horse races, sex, and other matters. Mostly I just listened and tried to act friendly and interested. We had wine and coffee with anisette in it, with the fellows chipping in to pay for the refreshments. (Doc would not let me pay my share on this first occasion.) As Doc had predicted, no one asked me about myself, but he told me later that when I went to the men's room there was an excited burst of conversation in Italian and that he had to assure them that I was not a G-man. He said he told them flatly that I was a friend of his, and they agreed to let it go at that.

We went several more times together to Chichi's gambling joint, and then the time came when I dared to go in alone. When I was greeted in a natural and friendly manner, I felt that I was now beginning to find a place for myself in Cornerville.

When Doc did not go off to the gambling joint, he spent his time hanging around Norton Street, and I began hanging with him. At first, Norton Street meant only a place to wait until I could go somewhere else. Gradually, as I got to know the men better, I found myself becoming one of the Norton Street gang.

As I began to meet the men of Cornerville, I also met a few of the girls. One girl I took to a church dance. The next morning the fellows on the street corner were asking me: "How's your steady girl?" This brought me up short. I learned that going to the girl's house was something that you just did not do unless you hoped to marry her. Fortunately, the girl and her family knew that I did not know the local customs, so they did not assume that I was thus committed. However, this was a useful warning. After this time, even though I found some Cornerville girls exceedingly attractive, I never went out with them except on a group basis, and I did not make any more home visits either.

As I began hanging about Cornerville, I found that I needed an explanation for myself and for my study. As long as I was with Doc and vouched for by him, no one asked me who I was or what I was doing. When I circulated in other groups or even among the Nortons without him, it was obvious that they were curious about me.

I began with a rather elaborate explanation. I was studying the social history of Cornerville—but I had a new angle. Instead of working from the past up to the present, I was seeking to get a thorough knowledge of present conditions and then work from present to past. I was quite pleased with this explanation at the time, but nobody else seemed to care for it. It was apparently too involved to mean anything to Cornerville people.

I soon found that people were developing their own explanation about me: I was writing a book about Cornerville. This might seem entirely too vague an explanation, and yet it sufficed. I found that my acceptance in the district depended on the personal relationships I developed far more than upon any explanations I might give. Whether it was a good thing to write a book about Cornerville depended entirely on people's opinions of me personally. If I was all right, then my project was all right; if I was no good, then no amount of explanation could convince them that the book was a good idea.

Of course people did not satisfy their curiosity about me simply by questions that they addressed to me directly. They turned to Doc, for example, and asked him about me. Doc then answered the questions and provided any reassurance that was needed.

I learned early in my Cornerville period the crucial importance of having the support of the key individuals in any groups or organizations I was studying. Instead of trying to explain myself to everyone, I found I was providing far more information about myself and my study to leaders such as Doc than I volunteered to the average corner boy. I always tried to give the impression that I was willing and eager to tell just as much about my study as anyone wished to know, but it was only with group leaders that I made a particular effort to provide really full information.

While I worked more closely with Doc than with any other individual, I always sought out the leader in whatever group I was studying. I wanted not only sponsorship from him but also more active collaboration with the study. Since these leaders had the sort of position in the community that enabled them to observe much better than followers what was going on and since they were in general more skillful observers than the followers, I found that I had much to learn from a more active collaboration with them.

I learned to take part in the street corner discussions on baseball and sex. This required no special training, since the topics seemed to be matters of almost universal interest. I was not able to participate so actively in discussions of horse-racing. I did begin to follow the races in a rather general and amateur way. I am sure it would have paid me to devote more study to the *Morning Telegraph* and other racing sheets, but my knowledge of baseball at least ensured that I would not be left out of the street corner conversations.

While I avoided expressing opinions on sensitive topics, I found that arguing on some matters was simply part of the social pattern and that one could hardly participate without joining in the argument. I often found myself involved in heated but good-natured arguments about the relative merits of certain major-league ball players and managers. Whenever a girl or a group of girls would walk down the street, the fellows on the corner would make mental notes and later would discuss their evaluations of the females. These evaluations would run largely in terms of shape, and here I was glad to argue that Mary had a better "build" than Anna, or vice versa. Of course, if any of the men on the corner happened to be personally attached to Mary or Anna, no searching comments would be made, and I, too, would avoid this topic.

Sometimes I wondered whether just hanging on the street corner was an active enough process to be dignified by the term "research." Perhaps I should be asking these men questions. However, one has to learn when to question and when not to question as well as what questions to ask.

I learned this lesson one night in the early months when I was with Doc in Chichi's gambling joint. A man from another part of the city was regaling us with a tale of the organization of gambling activity. I had been told that he had once been a very big gambling operator, and he talked knowingly about many interesting matters. He did most of the talking, but the others asked questions and threw in comments, so at length I began to feel that I must say something in order to be part of the group. I said: "I suppose the cops were all paid off?"

The gambler's jaw dropped. He glared at me. Then he denied vehemently that any policemen had been paid off and immediately switched the conversation to another subject. For the rest of that evening I felt very uncomfortable.

The next day Doc explained the lesson of the previous evening. "Go easy on that 'who,' 'what,' 'why,' 'when,' 'where' stuff, Bill. You ask those questions, and people will clam up on you. If people accept you, you can just hang around, and you'll learn the answers in the long run without even having to ask the questions."

I found that this was true. As I sat and listened, I learned the answers to questions that I would not even have had the sense to ask if I had been getting my information solely on an interviewing basis. I did not abandon questioning altogether, of course. I simply learned to judge the sensitiveness of the question and my relationship to the people so that I only asked a question in a sensitive area when I was sure that my relationship to the people involved was very solid.

$$*   *   *$$

At first I concentrated upon fitting into Cornerville, but a little later I had to face the question of how far I was to immerse myself in the life of the district. I bumped into that problem one evening as I was walking down the street with the Nortons [a group of young men from the neighborhood]. Trying to enter into the spirit of the small talk, I cut loose with a string of obscenities and profanity. The walk came to a momentary halt as they all stopped to look at me in surprise. Doc shook his head and said: "Bill, you're not supposed to talk like that. That doesn't sound like you."

I tried to explain that I was only using terms that were common on the street corner. Doc insisted, however, that I was different and that they wanted me to be that way.

This lesson went far beyond the use of obscenity and profanity. I learned that people did not expect me to be just like them; in fact, they were interested and pleased to find me different, just so long as I took a friendly interest in them. Therefore, I abandoned my efforts at complete immersion. My behavior was nevertheless affected by street corner life. When John Howard first came down from Harvard to join me in the Cornerville study, he noticed at once that I talked in Cornerville in a manner far different from that which I used at Harvard. This was not a matter of the use of profanity or obscenity, nor did I affect the use of ungrammatical expressions. I talked in the way that seemed natural to me, but what was natural in Cornerville was different from what was natural at Harvard. In Cornerville, I found myself putting much more animation into my speech, dropping terminal *g*'s, and using gestures much more actively.

As I became accepted by the Nortons and by several other groups, I tried to make myself pleasant enough so that people would be glad to have me around. And, at the same time, I tried to avoid influencing the group, because I wanted to study the situation as unaffected by my presence as possible. Thus, throughout my Cornerville stay, I avoided accepting office or leadership positions in any of the groups, with a single exception. At one time I was nominated as secretary of the Italian Community Club. My first impulse was to decline the nomination, but then I reflected that the secretary's job is normally considered simply a matter of dirty work—writing the minutes and handling the correspondence. I accepted and found that I could write a very full account of the progress of the meeting as it went on under the pretext of keeping notes for the minutes.

While I sought to avoid influencing individuals or groups, I tried to be helpful in the way a friend is expected to help in Cornerville. When one of the boys had to go downtown on an errand and wanted company, I went with him. When somebody was trying to get a job and had to write a letter about himself, I helped him to compose it, and so on. This sort of behavior presented no problem, but, when it came to the matter of handling money, it was not at all clear just how I should behave. Of course, I sought to spend money on my friends just as they did on me. But what about lending money? It is expected in such a district that a man will help out his friends whenever he can, and often the help needed is financial. I lent money on several occasions, but I always felt uneasy about it. Naturally, a man appreciates it at the time you lend him the money, but how does he feel later when the time has come to pay, and he is not able to do so? Perhaps he is embarrassed and tries to avoid your company. On such occasions I tried to reassure the individual and tell him that I knew he did not have it just then and that I was not worried about it. Or I even told him to forget about the debt altogether. But that did not wipe it off the books; the uneasiness remained. I learned that it is possible to do a favor for a friend and cause a strain in the relationship in the process.

I know no easy solution to this problem. I am sure there will be times when the researcher would be extremely ill advised to refuse to make a personal loan. On the other hand, I am convinced that, whatever his financial resources, he should not look for opportunities to lend money and should avoid doing so whenever he gracefully can.

If the researcher is trying to fit into more than one group, his fieldwork becomes more complicated. There may be times when the groups come into conflict with each other, and he will be expected to take a stand. There was a time in the spring of 1937 when the boys arranged a bowling match between the Nortons and the Italian Community Club. Doc bowled for the Nortons. Fortunately, my bowling at this time had not advanced to a point where I was in demand for either team, and I was able to sit on the sidelines. From there I tried to applaud impartially the good shots of both teams, although I am afraid it was evident that I was getting more enthusiasm into my cheers for the Nortons.

My first spring in Cornerville served to establish for me a firm position in the life of the district. I had only been there several weeks when Doc said to me: "You're just as much of a fixture around this street corner as that lamppost." Perhaps the greatest event signaling my acceptance on Norton Street was the baseball game that Mike Giovanni organized against the group of Norton Street boys in their late teens. It was the old men who had won glorious victories in the past against the rising youngsters. Mike assigned me to a regular position on the team, not a key position perhaps (I was stationed in right field), but at least I was there. When it was my turn to bat in the last half of the ninth inning, the score was tied, there were two outs, and the bases were loaded. As I reached down to pick up my bat, I heard some of the fellows suggesting to Mike that he ought to put in a pinch-hitter. Mike answered them in a loud voice that must have been meant for me: "No, I've got confidence in Bill Whyte. He'll come through in the clutch." So, with Mike's confidence to buck me up, I went up there, missed two swings, and then banged a hard grounder through the hole between second and short. At least that is where they told me it went. I was so busy getting down to first base that I did not know afterward whether I had reached there on an error or a base hit.

That night, when we went down for coffee, Danny presented me with a ring for being a regular fellow and a pretty good ball player. I was particularly impressed by the ring, for it had been made by hand. Danny had started with a clear amber die discarded from his crap game and over long hours had used his lighted cigarette to burn a hole through it and to round the corners so that it came out a heart shape on top. I assured the fellows that I would always treasure the ring.

Perhaps I should add that my game-winning base hit made the score 18-17, so it is evident that I was not the only one who had been hitting the ball. Still, it was a wonderful feeling to come through when they were counting on me, and it made me feel still more that I belonged on Norton Street.

Barbara Myerhoff

"So What Do You Want from Us Here?"

An anthropologist by training, Barbara Myerhoff began her field re-search career by studying the Huichol Indians of Mexico. But like many modern anthropologists she eventually turned to research settings within her own culture—in this case, elderly Jews who spent their days at a senior citizens' center in Venice Beach, California. She obtained a grant to explore the process of aging and to study the factors that give elderly people the strength to face such problems as poverty, neglect, loneli-ness, poor health, inadequate housing, and physical danger. For Myer-hoff, however, this was more than a research project; it was a return to her Jewish heritage, a search for roots.

The elderly folk of the Aliyah Senior Citizens' Center were former mi-grants from Eastern Europe who had few ties to their more assimilated offspring. Not only had they escaped the Holocaust, but many had out-lived their families and friends. The Center was their whole life. They constituted a subculture, a tiny group of survivors whose primary focus was on their Jewish heritage and its meaning in a difficult, unpredictable world. Myerhoff spent her days with them and came to know them inti-mately. In her ground-breaking book Number Our Days *she portrays them thinking, loving, arguing, and expressing themselves.*

In this selection Myerhoff describes the process through which she established her own identity as a researcher and developed a sense of balance between her concerns and those of the people she was observing. She also reveals an extraordinary sensitivity to the feelings of the elderly, a deep empathy with their efforts to overcome the obstacles facing them at every point in their day-to-day lives.

Myerhoff also developed a new awareness of the naturalness of aging, the fact that all of us will be old someday. "I see old people now in a new way, as part of me," she wrote, and she expressed gratitude at the opportunity to anticipate and contemplate her own future. Sadly, she did not live to become an elderly person herself; she died of cancer while still in her forties. However, her unique view of the elderly became legendary and has been an inspiration to numerous contemporary researchers.

I sat on the benches outside the Center and thought about how strange it was to be back in the neighborhood where sixteen years before I had lived and for a time had been a social worker with elderly citizens on public relief. Then the area was known as "Oshini Beach." The word *shini* still made me cringe. As a child I had been taunted with it. Like many second-generation Americans, I wasn't sure what being a Jew meant. When I was a child our family had avoided the words *Jew* and *Yid*. We were confused and embarrassed about our background. In public we lowered our voices when referring to "our people" or "one of us." My grandparents had also emigrated from an Eastern European *shtetl* as young people. Like so many of the Center folk, they, too, wanted their children to be Americans above all and were ashamed of being "greenhorns." They spoke to my parents in Yiddish and were answered in English. None of the children or grandchildren in the family received any religious education, yet they carried a strong if ambivalent identity as Jews. This identity took the form of fierce pride and defensiveness during the Holocaust, but even then did not result in any of us developing a clear conception of how to live in terms of our ethnic membership.

I had made no conscious decision to explore my roots or clarify the meaning of my origins. I was one of several anthropologists at the University of Southern California engaged in an examination of Ethnicity and Aging. At first I planned to study elderly Chicanos, since I had previously done fieldwork in Mexico. But in the early 1970s in urban America, ethnic groups were not welcoming curious outsiders, and people I approached kept asking me, "Why work with us? Why don't you study your own kind?" This was a new idea to me. I had not been trained for such a project. Anthropologists conventionally investigate exotic, remote, preliterate societies. But such groups are increasingly unavailable and often inhospitable. As a result, more and more anthropologists are finding themselves working at home these days. Inevitably, this creates problems with objectivity and identification, and I anticipated that I, too, would have my share of them if I studied the Center folk. But perhaps there would be advantages. There was no way that I could have anticipated the great impact of the study on my life.

In the beginning, I spent a great deal of time agonizing about how to label what I was doing—was it anthropology or a personal quest? I never fully resolved the question. I used many conventional anthropological methods and asked many typical questions, but when I had finished, I found my descriptions did not resemble most anthropological writings. Still, the results of the study would certainly have been different had I not been an anthropologist by training.

*   *   *

I followed the crowd inside and sat at the back of the warm, noisy room redolent with odors of fish and chicken soup, wondering how to introduce myself. It was decided for me. A woman sat down next to me who I soon learned was Basha. In a leisurely fashion, she appraised me. Uncomfortable, I smiled and said hello.

"You are not hungry?" she asked.

"No, thank you, I'm not," I answered.

"So, what brings you here?"

"I'm from the University of Southern California. I'm looking for a place to study how older Jews live in the city."

At the word *university,* she moved closer and nodded approvingly. "Are you Jewish?" she asked.

"Yes, I am."

"Are you married?" she persisted.

"Yes."

"You got children?"

"Yes, two boys, four and eight," I answered.

"Are you teaching them to be Jews?"

"I'm trying."

"So what do you want with us here?" asked Basha.

"Well, I want to understand your life, find out what it's like to be older and Jewish, what makes Jews different from other older people, if anything. I'm an anthropologist and we usually study people's cultures and societies. I think I would like to learn about this culture."

"And what will you do for us?" she asked me.

"I could teach a class in something people here are interested in—how older people live in other places, perhaps."

"Are you qualified to do this?" Basha shot me a suspicious glance.

"I have a Ph.D. and have taught in the university for a number of years, so I suppose I am qualified."

"You are a professor then? A little bit of a thing like you?" To my relief, she chuckled amiably. Perhaps I had passed my first rite of entrance into the group.

"Faegl, Faegl, come here!" Basha shouted to a friend across the room. Faegl picked her way neatly over to where we were sitting. She was wiry and slight as Basha was heavy and grand. "Faegl, sit down. Faegl, this here is . . . What did you say your name was? Barbara? This is Barbara. She is a professor and wants to study us. What do you think of that?"

"Why not? I wouldn't object. She could learn a lot. Are you Jewish?" Faegl leaned past Basha and carefully peered at me over her bifocals.

Basha accurately recited my qualifications and family characteristics. Faegl wasted no time. She moved over to sit next to me and began her interrogation.

"So you are an anthropologist. Then you study people's origins, yes? Tell me, is it true that human beings began in Africa once upon a time?"

"Many scholars think so," I answered.

"Ha! And once upon a time this country belonged to the Indians. That's right?" she went on.

"Yes, certainly," I answered.

"Now, a lot of people don't think it's right that we took away from them the country just because we were stronger, yes?"

"Yes." I was growing wary, sensing an entrapment.

Faegl continued systematically. "So this business about putting all the Arabs out of Israel because we said we had origins there, maybe that's not right either? It is not so simple, is it?"

"No, no. Certainly it is not simple," I answered.

"So Bashaleh, what do you say now?" Faegl asked her. "She's a professor and she says maybe it's not right. Like I told you, even from the Arabs we can't take away the land."

Basha looked at me closely while Faegl waited.

"You don't believe in *Eretz Yisroel* [the land of Israel; the promised land]?" she asked me. "You are some kind of anti-Semite?"

Faegl rescued me. "Basha! You think everyone who isn't a Zionist is an anti-Semite? Shame on you. You used to be an internationalist. You used to have beliefs."

Their argument had grown loud enough to attract attention. Abe, the director, came over to see what was going on. Again, Basha introduced me. I asked him about the possibility of doing my study here. He was noncommittal but friendly and after the lunch, we walked along the boardwalk together. He was exceptionally well-informed about the changes in the neighborhood during the last decade and a half. He seemed to know everyone on the streets, not only the elderly. But when he spoke of them, his voice was thick with affection, and anger at their being neglected. He evidently knew all the members, where they lived, how much money they had, where their families were, their state of mind and health, on an hour-by-hour basis.

*   *   *

For the next four years I was to be involved with these people, as an anthropologist, doing fieldwork, as a friend, and sometimes as a family member. When Josele Masada decided that I looked like his mother and told everyone I was his long-missing granddaughter, Barbarinka, no one was certain what to make of this, for boundaries between his memories, dreams, and the present were often blurred. Did he "really" think there was a biological bond between us, was this a wish, a metaphor, a great compliment? Since no one was certain of Masada's notion, our relationship could be neither affirmed nor denied, and it remained a puzzle to everyone, including me. I was right in expecting that my closeness to the subject would be both troublesome and advantageous, but there was no way I could have anticipated what the specific struggles and compensations would be.

The anthropologist engages in peculiar work. He or she tries to understand a different culture to the point of finding it to be intelligible, regardless of how strange it seems in comparison with one's own background. This is accomplished by attempting to experience the new culture from within, living in it for a time as a member, all the while maintaining sufficient detachment to observe and analyze it with some objectivity. This peculiar posture—being inside and outside at the same time—is called participant observation. This assumption of the natives' viewpoint, so to speak, is a means of knowing others through oneself, a professional technique that can be mastered fairly easily in the study of very different peoples. Working with one's own society, and more specifically, those of one's own ethnic and familiar heritage, is perilous, and much more difficult. Identifying with the "Other"—Indians, Chicanos, if one is Anglo, blacks if one is white, males if one is female—is an act of imagination, a means for discovering what one is not and will never be. Identifying with what one is now and will be someday is quite a different process.

In working among the elderly—also, I suspect, among the very young—an exceptionally important part of one's information is derived from nonverbal communication and identification, this because the bodily state is such a large determinant of well-being for the growing and declining organism. At various times, I consciously tried to heighten my awareness of the physical feeling state of the elderly by wearing stiff garden gloves to perform ordinary tasks, taking off my glasses and plugging my ears, slowing down my movements and sometimes by wearing the heaviest shoes I could find to the Center. Walking a few blocks to the day-old bakery in this condition became an unimaginably exhilarating achievement. Once by accident I stumbled slightly. The flash of actual terror I experienced was shocking. From the close watching of the elderly it seems I had acquired their assiduous need to avoid falling, though of course, to one my age in good health such a minor accident presents no real danger. This recognition occurred after I had been watching two very old women walk down the alley with great concentration, arms tightly linked, navigating impediments in slow-motion movements that were perfectly coordinated and mutually supportive. So great was their concern with balance they might have been walking a high wire.

As a society, we are increasingly cut off from the elderly. We do not have them in the midst of our daily lives, and consequently have no regular access to models of successful old age. How can we then do anything but dread the coming of age? I consider myself very fortunate in having had, through this work, an opportunity to anticipate, rehearse, and contemplate my own future. This has given a temporal integration to my life that seems to me an essential ingredient in the work of maturing.

*   *   *

In the beginning phases of my work with the elderly I suffered severe pangs of guilt. It took many forms and floated about, settling on different issues at different times. At first it focused on questions concerning my competence in the task I was embarking upon. Did I know enough Judaica? Did I know enough Yiddish? Was I too young? Was I too emotionally involved? Should I be working for the old people's welfare instead of studying them? and the like. In the course of a conversation with Shmuel, a very learned man who was to become one of my principal informants, I confessed my fears about not being able to do justice to the materials he was giving me. There was so much I did not understand. As usual, he was severe but not unfair in his response.

"You don't understand. How could you expect to understand? You ask me all these things, but you know nothing. You don't know Yiddish. You don't know Hebrew. You don't know Aramaic. You don't know Russian and not Polish. You have not set your eyes on any part of the place we lived in. How can you expect to understand?"

I agreed with him and was terribly discouraged. For a while, I stopped to study Yiddish, then realized that I was taking too much time out of the fieldwork. It was wasteful in view of the Center people's fluency in English. I also spent some time studying Jewish law and history, but the subjects were overwhelmingly complex, needing lifetimes of devotion to achieve more than a superficial understanding. I decided to try to follow the old people's leads in deciding what to study, learning as much as I could from them. I would enter these fields of knowledge in an *ad hoc* fashion, letting the elders point out what I needed to know as the work progressed rather than plowing into it systematically or for its own sake.

Resolving the question of my right to do the work did not free me from the inner and outer taunts. Many of the Center people continued to "make" me feel guilty. After greeting me warmly, Basha would often ask, "Never mind these other things you all the time ask about. Tell me, who's with your children?" Men and women alike would admire a new skirt or dress I wore, then turn over my hem for inspection. Nathan remarked, "For a lady professor, you don't do so good with a needle." When I stayed away too long, they scolded and snubbed me. When I was not completely fair (and sometimes even when I was) in the distribution of attention, I paid dearly for it. The old people were genuinely proud of me, generous, and affectionate, but at times their resentment spilled over. My presence was a continual reminder of many painful facts: that it should have been their own children there listening to their stories; that I had combined family and a career, opportunities that the women had longed for and never been allowed. And too, that I knew so little of their background suggested to them that they had failed to transmit to future generations any but fragments of their cherished past. I felt guilty about invading their privacy, for however much I explained my publication intentions, I knew our conversations sometimes crossed the invisible line from informed disclosure to inadvertent confidence. Diffuse and even irrational guilt plagued me until I had to laugh at myself. I had become a tasteless ethnic joke, paralyzed by Jewish guilt: about my relative youth and strength, about having a future where they did not, about my ability to come and go as I chose while they had to await my visits and my convenience, when I relished food that I knew they could not digest, when I slept soundly through the night warmed by my husband's body, knowing the old people were sleeping alone in cold rooms.

I considered quitting. It was unbearable to abide the countless ways in which the Center people used guilt, often unconsciously, intending not to hurt but only to make themselves feel potent. But after a time I accepted the fact that one cannot be "made" guilty. One volunteers. The arousal of guilt is what I have called "a strategy of intimacy," one of many used by the Center old people. Useless among strangers, it is based on interdependence and connectedness. The bright side of guilt is that it is an expression of a sense of responsibility for another's well-being. When I realized that, I became resigned and even grateful about my responses to my subjects.

I had been with these people for almost two years when I hit on what seemed the most significant component of my complex feelings about them. I chanced to read a comment by Isaac Bashevis Singer in *Enemies, A Love Story,* one of his novels about survivors. A single statement of his suddenly clarified matters for me. In reference to his own difficulties in writing about victims he remarked, "Although I did not have the privilege of going through the Hitler holocaust . . ." Yes, it was that feeling that they were set apart from the rest of us and hallowed by their suffering. Paradoxically they were the privileged ones for having lived on our behalf through what was in one sense our common fate. How, then, could anyone look at them dispassionately? How could I feel anything but awe and appreciation for their mere presence? In view of their proximity to mass destruction, it was indecent to ask more of them than that they be alive and in good spirits. But they were more than their sufferings; too great an appreciation on my part was a disservice and falsification, ultimately disrespectful. I wanted my people to be loved and admired as a result of my study, for in addition to being survivors, they were presently poor and maltreated. I wanted to protect them, even from my responses. But finally I accepted the necessity for sacrificing that desire. A reverential, protective attitude would allow the reader to distance him- or herself from them. The elders' accomplishments were important precisely because they were not heroes or saints, indeed this was one reason why they and the life they created were so colorful and appealing. Their flamboyance, humor, tendency to self-parody and self-criticism, their reaches for dignity and integrity, their occasional failures and lapses into foolishness, selfishness, and unkindness were part of what contributed to their success as survivors. My work would have to be a full-length portrait, light and darkness with more shading than sharp lines. Since neutrality was impossible and idealization undesirable, I settled on striving for balance. If these people emerged as real in their entire human range and variety, arousing admiration and disappointment, laughter and tears, hope and despair, I would be satisfied. My admiration for and gratitude to them must be evident. In the end, the only acceptable answer I could find to the question "Am I qualified to write this book?" was that my membership and my affection were my qualifications. When I judge these people, I judge myself.

Claire Sterk

Prostitution, Drug Use, and AIDS

Claire Sterk came to the United States from the Netherlands in 1986 as part of an exchange program between Erasmus University and the City University of New York's Center for Social Research. She had conducted research among prostitute and drug-using subcultures in the Netherlands for eight years. It was in the United States, however, that she became involved in AIDS research.

Sterk notes that in recent years there has been greater appreciation for ethnographic research as a means of providing background information for the evaluation of statistical data—that is, to find out about the people behind the facts. Populations "at risk" for AIDS—particularly prostitutes and intravenous drug users—constitute subcultures similar to those Sterk had studied in the past. They are best approached using the techniques of ethnographic research, especially observation and in-depth interviews. The use of these techniques allows the researcher to learn about sensitive issues that cannot be explored through more frequently used techniques such as questionnaires.

In the late 1980s Sterk conducted observational research in Newark, Jersey City, and New York City. The focus of her research was the behavior and attitudes of drug users and prostitutes, with emphasis on the impact of AIDS. Sterk was especially interested in discovering whether and to what extent women who become involved in prostitution through cocaine and crack use are at risk of contracting AIDS.

Although Sterk remains an outsider to the groups she is observing, her presence is accepted by members of those groups because she is "out there when they are out there"—in motels and hotels, brothels and escort services, shooting galleries and crack houses. She admits that she does not always feel safe in those environments (she is careful to ensure that a friend or colleague knows where she is); she also points out that safety depends largely on the attitude of the researcher: "These are human beings with feelings and emotions. If you care about them, they will care about you." During one two-month period she attended the funerals of seven women she knew from the street who had died of AIDS.

In this selection Sterk describes some of her experiences in the field and her feelings about them.

During the summer of 1986 I began conducting research among drug users and prostitutes in the New York metropolitan area. I had studied comparable groups in the Netherlands and was interested in discovering similarities and differences between the ways of life of these populations on both sides of the Atlantic Ocean. One can argue that turning tricks and shooting dope are the same all over the world. In reality, however, there are differences created by varying cultural circumstances. For example, in New York, where prostitution is illegal, the pimp plays a more important role in the prostitute's life than is the case in the Netherlands. When it comes to drugs, significant differences accrue from the fact that Dutch policies regarding drugs are more liberal than U.S. policies; moreover, crack has not yet become popular in the Netherlands.

Most of my research was done in Manhattan and Brooklyn and in northeastern New Jersey. Prostitutes and drug users frequently travel between New York and New Jersey. The two regions are close enough together so that the time it takes to travel between them amounts to less than thirty minutes. Operating in two adjacent states has advantages if one is involved in illegal activities; for one thing, it enables one to avoid an arrest warrant. If the police are seeking prostitutes in New York, the women simply shift their operation across the state line. Those living in New Jersey also cite economic reasons for commuting: In a large city like New York it is easier to make money, while the costs of living are significantly lower in New Jersey.

Before undertaking ethnographic research among people who are involved in deviant and very often illegal activities, one must locate the target population and determine how best to approach potential informants. With the help of colleagues, taxi drivers, and others, I was able to identify prostitute "strolls" and drug copping areas. I began visiting these neighborhoods and tried to get a sense of key events and characters by hanging out there. This gave me a chance to familiarize myself with the area while at the same time enabling the "regulars" to get to know my "face." Knowing where to go and recognizing faces, however, is only the beginning of a research effort. One can learn only so much through observation. The researcher must interact with the people he or she is studying.

A researcher—a stranger—cannot simply walk up to a potential informant and start chatting with him or her, especially if the informant is involved in illegal activities. When initiating a conversation, the researcher must justify his or her presence and indicate the desire for interaction, usually without knowing whether the other person can be trusted. Gaining trust is very important.

My acceptance into the prostitute subculture came about in a rather unexpected way. I had been walking around on the stroll for days and nobody wanted to talk to me. I recognized a few of the prostitutes from earlier visits, but they ignored me. But finally one of them, Ann, responded to my greeting. In a very cynical tone she asked me if I was looking for something special. For a second I did not know what to say. I answered very vaguely that I was just walking around. She thought this to be a silly answer and asked aggressively where I was from. I told her Amsterdam and started talking more openly. She teased me because I was getting red in the face. I kept on talking, glad that I had finally caught somebody's attention. I told her I was interested in prostitution and wanted to find out about the situation in the United States.

Ann challenged my knowledge, and apparently I answered her questions appropriately. She started talking about one of her girlfriends who was in "the life" and had moved to Europe with a boyfriend, an American GI stationed in West Germany. After the relationship ended, she began working in the sex business in Amsterdam. I was familiar with the club Ann mentioned and knew its owner. Ann began to open up and talk more to me, but she was careful. Another prostitute came by to check out what we were doing. Ann became very defensive about her relationship with me. She told the other woman to knock off, and described me as one of her friends.

I was fortunate, not only because Ann was willing to talk with me but also because I was not completely naive. Being somewhat familiar with the life style of the persons studied is of great value to a researcher in the field. The researcher will never have the knowledge of an insider without becoming a member of the group being studied, but a good ethnographer will try to find out about the norms and values of the world he or she is studying—always keeping in mind that too much knowledge might be seen as threatening.

In another situation I gained the confidence of an informant named Mo by demonstrating my knowledge of three-card monte, a popular con game. A white woman from Europe is not supposed to have such knowledge. My "showing off" made Goldman, a pimp, curious. Goldman, who has a penchant for big cars and lots of jewelry, said to me, "Damn, baby, you know what you are talking about. That's good, though; otherwise they would try to fool you. You have to prove yourself; showing off is what matters. Don't show off too much, now. We don't need wiseguys around here. I will tell you what to do and I will give my ladies instructions. If you are nice we won't have any problems."

While talking with potential informants, the researcher also develops a sense of who the important "players" are. It is necessary to gain their trust. They provide an entree into the community under study by facilitating the process of gaining the trust of others. Ideally, key contacts are individuals who are known and respected by other members of the community. Ann, for example, was one of the "main ladies"; Mo, a three-card monte player, was viewed as a good hustler; and Goldman was a well-known pimp.

During the initial stages of my research I was not the only one exploring and wondering. Respondents often tried to place me in impossible positions. Rumors spread that I was a potential prostitute, a drug user, or an undercover police officer. I was friendly, and so were my respondents, but simultaneously they were contemplating the possibility that I had a "hidden agenda." Mistrust and suspicion were ever-present, even in contacts with key respondents. Ann, for example, would, when I least expected it, ask me to repeat a certain story I had told her. She also explained to me that in trusting me she was taking chances herself. She would be blamed if it turned out that I could not be trusted, and this would have negative repercussions for her reputation.

One of the main lessons I have learned is that I must be honest and open about my intentions and that I must be constantly alert to the feelings of respondents. Being trusted does not assure acceptance. Again and again people challenged my presence and tested my intentions to "see if I was for real." Street life seems to require that one never develop permanent trust for anyone. One must continually check and reassess.

On one occasion I was standing on the street where the prostitutes were usually picked up by their customers. It was a nice evening, but business was slow. Pat, one of the streetwalkers, started telling me how they had been observing me. "We did not know if you were for real," she said. "It looked like we could trust you, but that could be your game. We decided to leave you alone and see how you would handle the tricks. I never forget the time the guy kept waving at you and you just looked around to see what we were doing. You couldn't have done better. He is still one of my regulars."

Pat and I now can laugh together about that situation. I referred the customer to her, telling him I was just hanging out on my night off.

There were many other episodes in which people tested my integrity, either by observing my reactions or by asking me for favors. The prostitutes would ask me to hold their purses, or they would share stories and check later to see if I had gossiped. They expected me to buy them a cup of coffee or a sandwich and to drive them around as if I were a cab driver. Ann advised me: "You have to be nice, but don't act like a softie!" I was also (unknowingly) used as "bait" for customers. Our tacit agreement was that I would not alienate the men who stopped to talk to me; instead, I would direct them to the "working girls."

Setting limits was a major issue. Repeatedly I had to convince drug users that I had no interest in buying stolen goods, and I often had to demonstrate to pimps that I was not interested in working for them. I was involved in the groups I was studying, but I remained an outsider in many ways. I was an outsider not only because I was not an active participant or because of my Dutch accent, but also because frequently I was one of the few, if not the only, white person in the area. This made me highly visible and easy to recognize. I was teasingly referred to as "the white girl," "Whitie," or "Miss Whitie," and one of the pimps told me he had a special deal for white ladies. The teasing had a bonding effect; several women expressed this by saying, "You are my only white friend" or "You are a nice white person."

During the many hours I spent with the prostitutes, of whom many were drug users, their pimps, drug partners, and dealers seldom interrupted their illegal activities because of my presence. Occasionally I was asked to leave the area because my presence was seen as a problem. The drug-using activities were generally covert and usually took place indoors, whereas the prostitution deals were more public.

Most of the women would talk with me about their work if I asked them about it, although they seldom discussed their work among themselves. (An exception was talk about tricks who could not be trusted or were too demanding.) Frequently they told me stories, mainly dealing with their emotions, that they did not share with one another. In short, I was treated as a trusted outsider who had a sense of what was going on in their lives.

My outsider status was validated on the occasions when I was seen as incompetent on the street. For example, everybody enjoyed my initial inability to anticipate police presence. I would be stopped and told to leave; my hidden audience would later make fun of me, but at the same time ensure that I didn't get into trouble. They also informed me about the dangers involved in being out on the street. "Prostitutes are not staying out late anymore," I was told. "A group of four young men have been coming into the area. They wait until it gets dark and start assaulting the women. The moment one of the women is alone, they jump on her, take her money, and hurt her."

The women became even more frightened after one of them was killed.

Paula said to me, "You should not come here after dark. We are from the street . . . I am not saying that I am stronger than you are, but you do not have to be out here. I won't come unless I have to. I am even storing dope so I don't have to go out late at night."

It was during these moments that I realized that I would always be an outsider. No matter how much time I spent with them, I could always return to another world, a world of safety and stability. I often felt bad about this, and about the fact that there was nothing I could do to change their situation. These feelings became stronger the more I was confronted with the consequences of the AIDS epidemic.

By now it is widely known that many groups besides homosexual males are at risk of contracting AIDS. Among those groups are intravenous drug users, sexually active individuals and their sexual partners, and their babies. In the New York metropolitan area infection rates among intravenous drug users are as high as they are among homosexual men. During the hours I spent talking with respondents, I tried to sensitize them to the risks they were taking, and we talked about the possibility of modifying their behavior. Condom use and needle sharing were frequent topics of discussion.

One evening I was sitting with three of the prostitutes. An outreach worker had visited the stroll and they had plenty of condoms. We were joking, but at the same time we were talking about safe sex. The women's opinions about condom use varied. Laura said she never used them. Cindy would not have sex without a condom, and Maria used condoms with her tricks but not with her boyfriend. Maria's boyfriend gets upset if she so much as shows him a condom. All three agreed that it is easier to propose the use of condoms with tricks than with steadies. But as Laura pointed out, "I'm not going to fight about it. What's the big deal? He'll turn around and find somebody else, if that's what he wants. I always check to see if they are clean anyhow."

Our conversation shifted to blow jobs. Their mood was playful but serious. Cindy told me to taste a rubber before I made any further comments. She has learned how to use a condom while having oral sex without the customer knowing it. She is very proud of this skill and provided a demonstration. Giggling, we tried to follow her instructions. I do not know if this made a lasting impression on Laura and Maria, but at least we brought the issue out into the open.

On another occasion one of the prostitutes, Angie, said that she didn't think using condoms made any difference. "I'm already in the gutter," she said. "I feel sick, am losing weight. I'm going to die anyhow. What fucking difference does it make?"

We talked about knowledge, attitudes, and behavior, and about the relevance of testing for HIV antibodies. Sometimes I initiated these discussions; at other times I was drawn into an ongoing conversation. The respondents could be divided into two groups. One stressed the importance of testing because it reveals the individual's current condition. Those who test negative are often motivated to change their behavior to avoid seroconverting; those who test positive can take steps to avoid spreading the virus. Another group opposed testing because there is no cure for AIDS. Their main question was, "What is the sense of getting tested if there is nothing you can do about it? It only fucks you up."

As a researcher, I had difficulty taking a stand on this issue. Generally I encouraged testing because of the respondents' involvement in risky behaviors.

Respondents who had tested positive for HIV antibodies wanted to discuss their status with me. Because we had already developed a relationship, they trusted me more than they would a "strange" counselor. Jacky, a 24-year-old street prostitute, confided in me: "I can't talk with them folks. They are straight or faggots and don't know what the hell they are talking about. I don't need a preacher telling me what to do. They better get their own act together. I'm scared and don't want to die. What am I going to tell my old man?"

AIDS changed the relationship between me and my respondents. I began to be seen as a sort of on-the-stroll counselor, even though I did not have a lot to offer besides listening and trying to make appropriate referrals. I remember one case in particular: that of Micky and Jeanne.

Micky was 32 years old; his girlfriend Jeanne was 26. They both injected drugs and smoked crack. Micky went out and "did his thing" to get cash, and Jeanne turned tricks when he did not have enough money to support both of them. Then Micky started feeling sick. He was so tired he could not work. Jeanne started working more hours while a friend of Micky's watched her back in exchange for some dope. Jeanne, Micky, and I spent a lot of time together. One day he started asking questions about AIDS. He was going to see a doctor because he felt very sick.

Three days later Jeanne told me he was in the hospital. He got very sick and an ambulance had to pick him up. She did not know what to do. A week later Micky was out on the street again. He refused to sign a form and the hospital "let him go" as soon as he could walk. While in the hospital Micky was tested for AIDS; he tested positive. He did not want to talk with a counselor.

I tried to persuade Micky and Jeanne to seek help, but they felt that no one understood them. They also wanted to continue to get high, each with their own syringe. Micky said, "I'm going to die and I want to enjoy things. I can make that decision myself." In a few months Micky died. Jeanne was never tested and went on working.

One of the ethical questions one faces as a researcher is what to do when an infected drug user continues to share hypodermic sets or an infected prostitute continues to have sex with her customers and/or boy-friend without using prophylactics. I frequently dealt with individuals who were seropositive but did not protect others against infection. One of them said to me, "They know as well as I do what the deal is. In this life everybody takes care of himself. If you want to take chances, it's your responsibility. I don't have to warn others."

My conversations with respondents about changing drug-using and sexual behaviors became more concrete as more people became sick and died of AIDS. The people who share a stroll or a copping area form a relatively closed community. Because of the visible effects of AIDS on members of the community, issues like drugs and sex came to be dis-cussed more openly. Almost everybody I spoke with knew the ways in which the AIDS virus can be spread, and conversations about the use of condoms and the sharing of "works" became more common. Increas-ingly, I was not the person who brought up these issues. Respondents came up to me and asked me questions, or simply wanted to talk about what was going on. The threat posed by AIDS to almost everybody in the community made people more open. It also made them feel more vulnerable. It is scary to see your buddies get sick and die.

The increasing number of friends and acquaintances dying of AIDS affected me deeply. Attending funerals became a way of showing my concern and respect. In one brief period six people from one research site died. I had known four of them fairly well and had interviewed the other two. The latter were street prostitutes who used drugs intrave-nously; the others included a drug-using prostitute, a male hustler, and two intravenous drug users, one female and the other male. All had lived in close proximity and had frequent dealings with one another. The so-cial linkages among them had been strong. Many of their friends had known all or some of them.

I was upset by the high rate of death among the people I was studying. I mentioned this to one of the women, who answered, "We all have this problem. It is going to get worse. Over half of the people around here are infected. Can you imagine . . . If you are out on the street long enough you learn to cope with everything. Getting sad or scared is not going to help. We have to survive. You have to set limits."

After this conversation I decided that things were getting out of hand. I discussed my feelings with several people, including colleagues and "field friends." In one neighborhood the situation had become so bad that children were referring to funeral cars as "AIDS wagons." But then something happened that made me realize that alongside of death there is always life.

A Hispanic woman, clearly ill, was trying to walk toward a nearby hospital. She was visibly pregnant. I approached her, and while we were talking her water broke. I realized that I didn't have time to get a car, so I jumped into the middle of the street and stopped the first car that came along. It was occupied by a middle-aged white couple. While I was explaining what was happening the woman groaned and said the baby, her second child, was coming. Although we were less than five minutes from the hospital, the baby was born in the back seat of the car. The woman in the front seat started crying and saying how thankful she was that we had chosen their car. The man walked away, sickened by the mess in the car. The mother, Carmen, cried and looked happily at her baby as she carried it into the hospital. I stood around, confused and disoriented. My clothes and hands were dirty. I was overwhelmed by having been involved in the birth of a baby on the same streets where people were dying of AIDS.

The AIDS epidemic has given ethnographic research a new dimension. AIDS has made me more aware of the fact that every researcher is affected by the work he or she does. One cannot remain neutral and uninvolved; even as an outsider, the researcher is part of the community under study and must recognize that fact.

William Kornblum

On Studying
South Chicago

*In the 1960s and 1970s a number of sociological studies focused on so-
cial stratification and politics in particular communities. Among them
was* Blue Collar Community, *William Kornblum's study of the steelworkers of South Chicago. Kornblum spent more than three years observing working-class politics—the politics of the trade union and the
local ward—in a community that had been dominated by heavy manufacturing for more than a century. He was attracted to South Chicago
not only by its dramatic labor struggles but also by its intricate ethnic
and communal life.*

*Although it lost much of its employment base in the late 1970s and
the 1980s, South Chicago remains a large steel mill community within
the city limits of metropolitan Chicago. Its population includes members
of almost every major ethnic and racial group that has settled in American industrial communities over the last century—Northern Europeans,
Eastern Europeans, Mexicans, and blacks. Although the European immigrants are often lumped together as "white ethnics," they are extremely diverse in cultural terms; the differing cultural backgrounds of
the more recent black and Mexican immigrants have also contributed to
the cultural complexity of this working-class community.*

Despite the cultural antagonisms of the different racial and ethnic groups that have settled in South Chicago, Kornblum found abundant evidence of worker solidarity as reflected in trade union activity and political loyalties. His observations impressed him with the strength and variety of the interpersonal networks formed by the leaders of different socioeconomic groups in an effort to aggregate their political power. Instead of a large number of alienated blue-collar workers, he found an intricate set of interconnected groups and coalitions that produced an unexpected degree of social cohesion.

During the time in which Kornblum was conducting his research, he and his wife lived in South Chicago and made many friends among their neighbors. He also participated actively in local political campaigns and was employed for six months as a subforeman in one of the area's steel mills. The steelworkers union president who found him the job told him it would allow him to "get a real education inside the mill." As the following selection shows, it certainly did.

In the initial stage of a community study the researcher frequently hesitates to make commitments. The choice of a specific set of research sites and questions, the selection of a place to live, a group of people to become friendly with, and a way of explaining one's purposes to residents, all seem like irreversible decisions. During this rather normal period of "hanging back" and surveying the diversity of people and situations, one is likely to feel extremely alien and isolated. Perhaps for this reason many fieldwork projects begin with the author seeking out a place to become known, one which advances familiarity with the people but does not necessitate lasting commitment. Thus in *Street Corner Society* William F. Whyte explains how he became friendly with the family of an Italian restauranteur who provided him with a congenial base from which to plan his further participation in the community's life. Following this precedent I found a Serbian immigrant restaurant run by an enormous peasant woman and her very slight husband. Radmilla and Mike appreciated my halting attempts to converse with them in Serbo-Croatian, and they introduced me to the establishment's regulars. The majority of the patrons were Serbian immigrant men in their mid-thirties to early forties. Almost all were steelworkers. On Friday and Saturday nights they filled the restaurant to eat, drink, and dance to the popular music of contemporary Serbia.

One Friday night I entered in the middle of a brawl, which I learned was the continuation of an argument started in the steel mill three blocks away. While the electric guitar and accordion ensemble played on, three or four men were shouting in Serbo-Croatian and pushing each other. At this point Radmilla, who weighed at least 250 pounds, stepped into the crowd to separate the antagonists. As she did this, a man named Stanko seized a bar stool but she pushed him away easily. Infuriated, he threw the stool at her husband, Mike, who had had just enough to drink that he did not duck in time and was struck on the head and shoulders. In the ensuing melee I tended to the fallen Mike while Radmilla cleared the tavern and restored calm. After that evening I became a welcome friend in their tavern and I felt I had found a place where I did belong in the community. It soon became apparent, however, that I was viewing the ethnic group and the community from one of its most peripheral social circles.

Although it was a congenial spot to stop on my visits to South Chicago, most of the patrons at the Neretva Lounge were among the most recent arrivals to the city from Serbia. As such they were generally men without families, or whose families had remained in Yugoslavia. Along with an assortment of non-Serbian alcoholics and a few transient Mexicans the group was quite distant from the more established networks of South Chicago Serbian ethnicity. Socially they were even farther from the networks of people who involved themselves in the life of the larger community. The people at the Neretva were somewhat involved with other Serbian groups in establishing a new Serbian church. Since they had broken away from the church established by the pioneer generation of Serbian settlers, there was a great deal of tension in the relationships between these factions. The native-born Serbians and Croatians referred to the immigrants as DP's while their own ethnic identity and social institutions seemed to me to be largely the product of their experience in South Chicago and other industrial communities of this society. To learn more about the differences between native-born and immigrant South Slavs, I began spending more time among native-born Serbian and Croatian residents. Thus at the end of 1967 I began looking for a place to settle in the community.

As I began hunting for an apartment, it became clear why I had chosen to study this community rather than other South Slavic neighborhoods elsewhere in the metropolitan area. South Chicago fascinated me. I had never seen such heavy industry at close range, and I was awed by the immensity of the steel mills and the complexity of the water and rail arteries which crisscrossed the area's neighborhoods. I saw more of the spectrum of cultural groups which had settled and built the community. Thus, I was beginning to see that my study would have to concern itself as much with the larger community as it would with the cultural and social adaptations of Serbian and Croatian settlers. In the impressive series of community studies compiled by Chicago sociologists there were none which explicitly focused on this type of community. Therefore, I came to feel that in addition to studying the cultural and social adaptations of South Slavic people, my work should also include material on this important industrial community.

This was also the period of increasingly bitter sentiment against the war in Indochina. Campus political groups were continually debating the issue of how to involve "the working class" in antiwar activities, or if such a task could be accomplished at all. Surprisingly few of my university friends had any knowledge even of the working-class communities nearest to the University of Chicago. Mention of the fact that I was spending time in the steel mill neighborhoods of South Chicago often brought the response, "Oh, you mean all those neighborhoods around Gary?" Chicago's mill neighborhoods begin on 79th Street, just nineteen blocks from the university, but they are often perceived as being closer to Gary, more than thirty miles to the south. Indeed, the blue collar neighborhoods which begin in South Chicago bear great similarity to those continuing past Gary to South Bend, Indiana. I thus resolved that whatever else it accomplished, my study should attempt to show what life is like in such places. It should show what political questions actually do challenge the residents, and among these would likely be the issue of working-class race relations.

In March 1968 my wife and I moved into a tenement flat in Irondale, one of the oldest neighborhoods of first settlement in the community. Irondale was a logical choice for a number of reasons. First, it had been one of the most popular neighborhoods for South Slavic immigrant settlement earlier in the century. It still retained a significant population of older settlers plus an increasing number of younger "DP" families. Second, it had been the site of the severe racial rioting which I read about in Frank London Brown's novel *Trumbull Park*. The late black author had vividly described the awful experience of trying to survive (with his family) in the neighborhood's housing project. Fourteen years had passed since these riots, but they were well remembered in Chicago. I suspected, rightly as it turned out, that we would be living among many of the people who had done the rioting. We would have a chance to see the issues from their perspective and learn how the intervening years had softened their violently defensive behavior. What I did not fully understand, however, was that Irondale was also becoming a Mexican neighborhood. In various ways the Mexicans were acting as a transition group to the eventual settlement of more black families in the neighborhood.

Irondale's older white families continued to be extremely sensitive to racial issues and bitterly opposed to racial integration of their neighborhood. Since I was then meeting many of the leaders of the violent resistance that had occurred in the Trumbull Park riots, I was also coming in for a good deal of scrutiny and suspicion. Although I wanted to get to know the central figures in the South Deering Improvement Association, this was not a simple matter for an outsider. If I was to hear how these men and women felt about the Trumbull Park riots, I would need greater access to their private haunts, especially the basement of the American Legion Hall, where the association had a bar that was off limits to the public.

Fortunately, as an ethnographer I am blessed with a unique asset: a wife with a quick wit, a ready laugh, a genuine interest in other people, and a willingness to come with me on almost any adventure. One day I informed her that I had volunteered the two of us to work for the Improvement Association at its food stands at the July 4 Trumbull Park Festival. We worked all day cooking and serving grinder sandwiches, and all the key members of the Association worked with us. It soon became clear that Susan was a master of mental arithmetic and could make change in an instant with no mistakes. I, on the other hand, had a strong back and was good for hauling boxes of food and soft drinks. All day Susan cracked jokes with the neighbors and with the leaders of the Improvement Association. At the end of the day we were invited to the private bar, where Susan was given the honor of assisting in counting the money and was then invited to take a hand in the poker game. I served as a friendly and clearly nonthreatening onlooker.

After that occasion we were accepted everywhere in the neighborhood. When Susan was expecting our first child, our popularity with many of the women in the neighborhood increased even further, and we were increasingly invited to major social affairs like weddings and large union gatherings. That Thanksgiving we received not one but two free turkeys, one from the ward political organization, via the neighborhood precinct captain, and one from the local church (since our part of the neighborhood was quite the poorest section).

When our first child was born, after a year in Irondale, we began spending a great deal of time with our Mexican neighbors because they were more likely to have young children than our somewhat older South Slavic and Italian neighbors. From them, and especially from the Mexican youth groups which hung out on our corner, I learned that there was continual conflict with the Mexicans from the Millgate and Bessemer Park neighborhoods on the other side of the community. Similar to the opposition which existed between native-born and immigrant South Slavic groups, this opposition between the Mexican neighborhoods conformed quite closely to the pattern of "ordered segmentation" which Gerald Suttles analyzed in *The Social Order of the Slum*. The first level of opposition or conflict between ethnic groups in the community did not involve different cultural groups but occurred among equivalent territorial groups of the same ethnicity.

The next level of opposition tended to unify diverse groups from Irondale against those in geographically separated neighborhoods such as the

East Side. On the other hand, all the residents whom I spoke to referred to the entire area as South Chicago, and they considered themselves residents of that community.

This perception seemed somewhat paradoxical. On the one hand so many people I met were generally involved in provincial feuding within their ethnic groups, and on the other they were in various ways quite clearly becoming involved in the life of the larger community. To investigate this problem it again seemed important to become familiar with the way the larger industrial and political institutions of the community operated. In particular it would be necessary to understand how experiences in the steel mills, the labor unions, and the political institutions of the community in various ways modified the residents' notions of which groups and individuals are worthy of their trust. In answering these questions I believed I would also begin to understand the processes whereby so many cultural groups had learned not only to coexist with each other but to adjust their basic patterns of ethnic social organization to compete in the class and status systems of the community and the larger society. From the start of my work I had been meeting and interviewing people whom I identified as leaders of various cultural and political institutions in the community. It appeared that I would need to follow their activities at a much closer range.

Soon after moving into the community I had begun a systematic effort to attend any and all public meetings in the community, to identify local leaders, and to arrange to meet with them for an introduction or a formal interview. Before long I learned to resist the "compulsion to confess" which often troubles field researchers. Most people I met in the course of my daily life were interested in why I had settled in the community. In answering this question I explained that I was teaching at the nearby University of Indiana, Hammond extension, while my wife was a student at the University of Illinois Circle Campus in the central city. The Irondale location was a halfway point for both of us. This was true, and although it omitted my main motives for settling in South Chicago, it made routine social intercourse much easier. If to every tavern clique and candy store acquaintance I had divulged my intentions to study the community, I would have probably elicited some parody of life in sociological jargon. But when I introduced myself to specific residents of the community, or whenever I interviewed someone, I attempted to explain the goals of my study as simply and consistently as I could, and the interview would generally proceed without misunderstanding of my goals.

Gradually, through these introductions and interviews I began to become friendly with a rather large number of political activists and neighborhood leaders. After introducing myself to a local labor leader, for example, I would then find myself meeting that person during my regular round of visits to public places and community events. These encounters would lead to new introductions and greater familiarity. By the end of my first year in South Chicago I counted well over fifty persons who had expressed interest in my study and were in various ways providing me with information about the underlying meaning of the political and social events I observed. Among the circles in which I was becoming more or less accepted were a group of Italian and Serbian steelworkers from Irondale who ran the local union at one of the area's large mills, a group of younger political activists from the East Side who met regularly to discuss community events and to plan political activities, two groups of ward political activists of mixed ethnicity, and friendship groups which met regularly in about fifteen taverns where I made rounds.

In addition to participating in the informal life of these groups I attended as many functions of the Serbian and Croatian ethnic groups as possible. Also, through the normal course of life among my Mexican neighbors I had many opportunities to observe the culture and social organization of Mexican neighborhood ethnic groups. Fieldwork was becoming more than a full-time occupation, and I often found myself dictating slurred field notes at 4:00 A.M. after a full day of meetings and social drinking in the area's taverns and political clubs. Despite the full schedule I had developed, I began to feel that the more I learned about the community through my friends and informants, the more necessary it was for me to commit myself to a greater degree to South Chicago's life style. I felt like a knowledgeable outsider who was missing some of the most important experiences of life in the community. At this time, in the middle of my second year of fieldwork in South Chicago, a friend whose opinion I highly valued, the Serbian president of a local steel union, confronted me with a serious challenge. "How can you really understand what goes on here," he asked, "if you've never spent any time inside a steel mill?" I replied that it had been my desire to work in a mill, that I agreed it was necessary, but when I had applied to work in one of the area's large mills a few months earlier I had been turned down because I had "too much education to push a broom in a laborer's job." Amused, my unionist friend asked me if I would like a job in the mill he represented. He assured me that he would arrange things so that my job would allow me to "get a real education inside the mill." Before I was given the job my friend called me one night to ask, "Bill, you're not one of these SDS guys, are you? You know there's a lot of talk these days about radicals coming into the mills to stir up trouble." I assured him that such was not my intention and within another week I was hired as a subforeman.

I approached my job in the mill with some embarassment. As a subforeman I was nonetheless a representative of management when most of my sympathies and many of my friendships were with rank-and-file workers. Outside the mills, in social circles frequented by steelworkers and their families, one rarely met any foremen or managerial officials, and indeed management was often spoken of with some disdain. Also, as a foreman I was not allowed to perform manual work since the union viewed that as an encroachment on workers' jobs in the plant. My job was to oversee and coordinate the work of about thirty men who were chippers, laborers, machine operators, cranemen, and loaders. As the men taught me how to accomplish my work with a minimum of conflict and disruption of their normal institutional arrangements with each other and with management, I began to see that my friend had situated me in a difficult job but one which was about the best position a sociologist could have had.

In performing my duties as subforeman I had to understand how the work on my end of the mill fit into the overall division of labor in the entire plant. As a managerial employee I could circulate relatively freely throughout the mill to learn how steel was produced and to converse informally with workers in hundreds of different occupations. Since mine was the lowest status managerial position possible, I represented little threat to anyone. Most of my rank-and-file peers were making more money than I was, and, as they delighted in pointing out, their jobs did not include the headache of being responsible to higher level managerial officials. In reflecting on the differences between my low level managerial position and the more narrowly circumscribed activities of the rank-and-file workers with whom I spent the bulk of my time, I began to understand from a personal viewpoint more of the meaning of unionism and labor bargaining for the average steelworker.

The other foremen with whom I worked were much more concerned about pleasing their superiors than were the rank-and-file workers. The latter were guaranteed advancement through the seniority system as long as they learned their jobs and performed them reliably. In case of trouble the workers could turn to their grievancemen and the union officials they had elected to intercede on their behalf in their dealings with management. The foremen had none of this protection. Although they claimed they did not need it, and indeed the vast majority of their superiors were considerate, experienced men, their occupational culture was full of stories of ambitious young foremen who had crossed high level officials at the wrong time and had been set back in their careers. None of our superiors in the rolling mill were vindictive types, but I was warned that Mr. W____, a high level manager who circulated throughout the entire plant, should be carefully avoided when he came into our mill.

Shortly thereafter, during a week when my turn was working nights, my general foreman warned me that the feared W____ had been seen leaving the adjacent mill heading in the direction of my work area. I was advised to make sure my men were all working properly and then to go off on an errand elsewhere in the mill. Here I should note that company officials were not aware of my intention to write about mill work. I rationalized this situation by attempting to do my job so that my personal motives for being in the mill would not compromise the performance of my work. On this occasion, however, I did not heed the older foreman's well-intentioned advice. Instead I loitered in my work area to see for myself what an encounter with W_____ would be like. When he entered my area of the mill, he walked directly up to me. Without introducing himself, he barked a question which produced the following dialogue:

W: What's that steel being loaded into those cars?

Kornblum: Oh, that's a mixed order of spring steel and thirty foot rounds that we're trying to load before the switch comes in.

W: I can see what it is. Who is it for? Where's it going?

Kornblum: Well, let's see, I think it's for . . .

W: God dammit. Do you know who that steel is for or don't you?

Kornblum: I'm not sure.

W: You damn well better get off your dead cock and find out what's being done around here or you're not going to last. This is a steel mill and not a nursery school. We've got too many jagg offs like you who sit around with their thumbs up their assholes and don't know what's going on.

The official strode away leaving me trembling with anger and humiliation. I had worked in many blue collar jobs before entering the steel mill, and as a laborer on an East River construction dock in Manhattan I had seen corruption and violence which made the normal routine of mill work seem tame. Since I was doing a relatively good job as a new foreman in a mill beset with serious racial and ethnic cleavages, I did not believe I should be treated in this way by someone who had never seen me before. It is true that I should have known the answer to his question and he was justified in "chewing me out." But except in jest the foremen on the shop floor rarely spoke to their own men in such terms. The dictates of common sense and the watchful influence of union representatives usually prevented such confrontations between foremen and workers. In general such personal experiences as this made me a good deal more sensitive to the style and content of interactions in the mill and deepened my desire to understand the meaning of unionism in the context of my study. Thus I pursued this goal while I worked in the mill and later when I assisted my unionist friends in their political campaigns.

Many sociologists have regarded "informal organization" as an inevitable characteristic of industrial bureaucracies, but one which in the interest of rationality and productivity must be manipulated through the techniques of "industrial relations." Given the orientation of my research I could not view the issue in this way. The study of informal relations among the workers became another aspect of my inquiry into how steel production creates an occupational community inside the mill. I thus attempted to discover the conditions under which revelations of character on the job could be as important as ethnic and racial categories in guiding the workers' behavior. My run-in with W_____, for example, immediately became the subject of gossip and bantering in work groups throughout the mill. "How could a kid with your education act like such a dummy?" asked the chief loader. This question launched a long philosophical discussion in the loaders' shanty. Most of the loaders worried that the incident would hurt my chances for advancement in the company. Others suggested that it should make me question the desirability of holding a job with management. Finally, a young Mexican loader, who was also a friend from the neighborhood, settled the argument in a statement which has remained in the front of my mind ever since. "What you guys don't understand," he stated, "is that Kornblum isn't stuck here like most of us stiffs. In his life he can do just about anything he really wants to do." Although perhaps somewhat obvious, this insight made me much more sensitive to the workers' attempts to express their own individuality throughout their careers in the steel mill. I also understood another side of this remark from my own difficulties in attempting to carry on my other fieldwork while remaining in the mill.

One morning after I had been working in the mill for almost six months I boarded a bus with a large group of Tenth Ward Spanish Speaking Democrats to attend the Chicago Democratic Day at the Illinois State Fair in Springfield. Since I had worked the previous night turn I immediately fell asleep. When I awoke about an hour later everyone on the bus was laughing at me. One of my neighbors had told those who did not know me that I was a worker at the Ford assembly plant down the road from our steel mill. He explained that I had fallen asleep and missed my stop. Some of South Chicago's Mexican activists still jokingly refer to me as "the guy from the Ford plant." This Springfield outing ended back in South Chicago about fifteen minutes before my shift began again in the mill. After eight hours of seeking places to steal a few minutes' sleep, I realized that I was reaching a point of diminishing returns in my participation inside the mill. Political events were rapidly accelerating in the outside community, and I could not become as involved in them as I wished because of the severe physical and temporal demands of mill work.

From the beginning of the research I had followed political campaigns and the careers of local politicians quite closely. At first I had attended meetings of campaign workers on both sides of the factional disputes in the community, thereby developing a large number of informants who supplied me with details of events I had witnessed. Generally it was necessary to compare carefully the accounts of a number of informants in order to compensate for individual biases and personal perceptions. At the same time I was beginning to feel that I had accumulated personal debts to many local groups, especially to my unionist friends and to many of my Slavic and Mexican neighbors. Working in the mill had brought me much more general acceptance in the community, but acceptance also subjected me to the same pressures to commit myself in partisan campaigns that others felt.

The pressure to become committed to other people is a general characteristic of community life in South Chicago, but during the time I lived in the community this pressure was probably as great as it had ever been. This was a time when the community was involved in sorting out the leadership of its most central institutions. For this reason all my friends and informants found themselves in one way or another drawn into competition between aggregations of community groups. It seemed that only the most financially secure or socially marginal people could afford not to take sides. This same spirit of partisanship also affected me. I began to feel that I could not remain aloof from political commitment when all the people I cared for had so much more at stake than I did. Aside from the personal aspect of this decision, there are very real limitations to what one can learn about political processes through informants. If one wishes actually to watch decisions being made in a competitive political system, it is often necessary to become part of the decision-making body itself. I did this by taking highly partisan, although "behind the scenes" roles in political campaigns.

The liabilities of this strategy are numerous and deserve some attention. First, it is obvious that the more committed one is to a particular faction, the less one can learn, at first hand, about others. This may not be quite so true in higher levels of political competition where political expertise is more rationally calculated and more often bought and sold, but it is certainly the case in community politics. Even though the competition is highly institutionalized, when neighbors and workmates compete against each other, careful attention is paid to one's affiliations, and trust is easily jeopardized. In consequence of this, whenever I committed myself to a given faction I attempted to function as much as possible in capacities which would require little public exposure. In order to keep up with events in opposing factions I attempted to explain my affiliations as frankly as possible to friends on opposite sides, in much the same terms as any other resident of the community would. In this way it was possible to act as a partisan and still communicate with friends in opposing factions who acted as my informants. Here the amount of time spent in fieldwork was extremely important. I did not become actively committed until the third year of my research. By that time I had friends throughout the community who could understand, if not always agree with my partisanship.

Another problem in taking on partisan roles as a researcher is that it almost inevitably causes bias in favor of those to whom one is committed. In my case, again, the answer to this problem was to maintain close informants on opposing sides, and to try, in the analysis of events, to be on guard against my own partialities so that I might correct them or use them knowingly. It is also true that by taking on activist roles the researcher's own actions may alter the situation. Aside from the problems of analysis which this presents, it may also draw one into further commitment. For example, in becoming involved with South Chicago political leaders, and especially with unionist politicians, I began to feel responsible for the future. Once having taken an active part in political competition, I no longer felt that my relationship with the community would end when the study was completed.

Part IV

The Observer's Role

The right and privilege of being an observer is a gift presented to the researcher by his host and subjects. . . . The gift of access, of witnessing social life as it is lived in someone else's environment, exercises a tyranny of its own.

Charles Bosk

Edmundo Morales

Researching Peasants and Drug Producers

The Peruvian-born sociologist Edmundo Morales has conducted extensive research on narcotics and substance abuse, with particular emphasis on cocaine production and trafficking. In 1983 he decided to return to his native region in the Andes Mountains to explore the changes that had occurred there as a result of the shift of the local economy toward the production and processing of cocaine for export. For cocaine and its derivatives, often known as "white gold," have become the drugs of the 1980s, and in Peru the new cocaine economy has displaced the former Andean coca trade.

In the course of his research, Morales discovered that the peasants of the Andes villages had become dependent on the worldwide traffic in cocaine. Most of them worked for several months each year in coca-processing laboratories hidden in the jungle. Others sold meat to the managers of the cocaine factories. Morales was dismayed to see so much food being diverted to the jungles from the impoverished highlands. Although the peasants were gaining cash income, they were also becoming addicted to cocaine and were ignoring the need for more important social changes in their own villages.

The purpose of Morales's study was to identify alternative means of making a living for peasants who support themselves by participating in the cocaine economy. To do so, Morales needed to analyze the social,

This selection is adapted from Edmundo Morales, *Cocaine: White Gold Rush in Peru* (Tucson: University of Arizona Press, 1989).

*cultural, economic, and political meaning of the cocaine industry—an
immense task, despite his knowledge of the Quechua language and his
familiarity with the culture of the people he was studying. He spent several summers visiting and interviewing the people of the highlands, often
experiencing unexpected hardships. Some of those hardships are described in this selection from his book,* Cocaine: White Gold Rush in
Peru, *which was published in 1989. The selection also addresses the issues and dangers confronting a researcher who is observing people engaging in illegal activities.*

During a visit to my hometown in the spring of 1980, I decided to do
what a professor in college had advised me: "Go back home and look
into the changes in the community." Neither during my childhood nor
in numerous visits back had I ventured outside the boundaries of my
native community, Llamellín. In my youth, I was part of the indigenous
culture and, as an adult visitor, I lacked the skills to make sense of the
obvious. Becoming an ethnographer of the Andes, native though I was,
was a long process, for learning from or observing other people whose
culture and society is the same as one's own roots I found very difficult
and possible only when a disciplined approach was incorporated into my
everyday routine.

On my exploratory trip in 1980, the first thing I did when I arrived in
the district capital of Llamellín was to look for a companion who was
familiar with the route and the area. A local photographer volunteered
for the trip. The next step was to rent a horse or a mule for transportation, and prepare a *fiambre,* provision consisting of two guinea pigs,
toasted maize, and some homemade bread for at least two days' travel.
My companion and I left town and headed for Paras, the community of
my first fieldwork.

After thirteen hours of tedious horseback riding, we followed the rec-
ommendation of a teacher we had met on our way and stopped in one
of the five villages of Paras. At the church of San Martín, we washed
our hands and watered our horses. Directly across from the church was
a house with Coca-Cola posters on the door. We knocked on the door
but there was no answer. Through the next door of the same house we
heard voices. Someone noticed us and came out to ask what we wanted.
He was drunk. We told him that we only wanted a bottle of Coca-Cola,
to which he answered that all he had was alcohol and alcohol was as
good as cold water. We had run out of boiled drinking water and had to
try to find something to satisfy our thirst. He asked our names and we
asked his. We found out that he was the lieutenant governor *(teniente
gobernador)* for the five villages of Paras. Assuming that he would use
his influence, we asked him to recommend someone in the community

to give us shelter for at least one night. He went into the room where the rest of his friends were discussing their plans. Shortly thereafter six drunken peasants stood before us.

They introduced themselves by their titles. They were the members of the central committee of the community. Each of them asked us questions about our identity, profession, and especially the purpose of our visit to Paras. They wanted me to show them some kind of letter of introduction or at least a personal identification card bearing my picture and my name, or even a calling card from any provincial authority introducing me to the community. I had nothing, not even my school identification card. I explained my presence and purposes to them over and over and begged them to believe me. They would not accept the excuse that I had left all my documents in Llamellín, nor would they believe that I had been born and raised in the province.

Since I could not provide identification, they asked us "kindly and immediately" to leave the village. It was getting dark and we had nowhere to go. Suddenly the president of the Administrative Council addressed my companion and said, "I think I know you." My companion presented his identification as a photographer, but I remained a problem. They invited us to have a drink before leaving the village and we accepted. My companion and I drank the alcohol, smiling and looking at the Coca-Cola poster. At this point I asked the peasants to let me take their picture. They liked the idea of posing as members of the central committee. Almost in unison they said, "Yes, my engineer." Then they wanted me to pose with them for another frame. Right after my assistant snapped the camera, I suggested we have another drink and offered to pay for it. "Correct, my engineer," they answered. By the time we had emptied the bottle we all were friends, and the same person who had asked us to leave the village offered us his humble home for as long as we wanted to stay in Paras. He hoped it would be a long stay.

The Solis family gave us the best room they had, which apparently had been unoccupied for some time. We used the only steel bedstead they had. Our bed linen consisted of four sheepskins and two wool quilts infested with fleas and lice which made our nights interminable. One day before we left the village the Solis family killed a pig to give us a farewell lunch. They assigned us their best mules for our transportation back to Llamellín and one of them even walked for about one hour with us up to the point where the broad trail began that would make our return easier.

Aside from the first day of difficulty, I had no problem at all as a visitor in Paras. There was some hesitation when I presented myself as a sociology graduate student from New York and spoke to them in Quechua. However, as they listened to me speaking to them in terms that only a native could understand, telling them jokes and fairy tales, they gave broad smiles as a sign of accepting their visitor. From then on, they acted friendly and were responsive and cooperative. I entered their lives and functioned almost as one of them. Good humor, patience, and the bottle of alcohol spent on the first day produced excellent returns.

*   *   *

In the spring of 1981, about one month before my trip from New York, I asked the chairperson of my committee to sign a letter in Spanish addressed to the head of the police, the subprefecto, the mayor, the judge of First Instance, and the director of education of the Province. In Lima, I obtained a letter of introduction from the American Embassy wherein the cultural attache stated the purpose of my stay in Peru; this letter opened the doors of public libraries (there are not many of them), universities, museums, and so forth.

Once in the capital town of the province to which Paras belongs, I paid formal visits to the authorities to whom the letter from my mentor had been directed. The authorities, in turn, had already sent a transcription of the letter to their representatives in other towns announcing my presence and asking them for cooperation in the research.

When I arrived in Illauro, the village of my residence during fieldwork, the local teacher whom I had met a year before was expecting me. He had already rented a one-room house for me near the school building where he lived. He had my room cleaned by his students and borrowed a bedstead, sheepskins, quilts, and a table from various families. I had taken my own sleeping bag. Despite my experience the year before with lice and fleas, I failed to bring with me any insecticides, so pediculosis was inevitable.

The next morning I was having breakfast when a delegation of authorities from the village of San Martín came to welcome me and, at the same time, invite me once again to live in their village. I explained to them that I had not come exclusively to spend my time in Illauro or any of the five villages. I said I would be visiting every family I could, and that the only reason I had settled in Illauro was that the local teacher had rented a house for me there. When they knew the location of my house, which lay about twenty-five steps from a young, attractive widow's house, they smiled, wished me luck, and left.

The first person I had planned to visit was the village leader who, during my previous visit, had offered me full cooperation and who I thought would be my key informant. He had changed his mind and refused to cooperate. He advised me to pick another community to avoid problems with the local people. He had secretly started warning his co-villagers of the danger of my presence in Paras owing to my "identification with the other party." He also urged them to expel me from the community, for I had no official authorization to stay in Paras. He did not know that I had been authorized by the provincial authorities to do research, and he was surprised when he learned that I had been cleared in every respect. My research project became more and more challenging.

It had first been my plan to collect historical and political data, but as a result of the visit to the leader I decided to start immediately interviewing and observing the people. No one resisted. Fortunately, when I went back to Llamellín after staying two weeks in Paras, I met an Aprista congressman visiting the province who had already been informed of my project. The congressman asked me to join him at a lunch where he was to be a guest of the notables of Llamellín. After lunch, while we were still talking, the leader who had tried to create difficulties for me knocked on the door. He came to urge the congressman to visit Paras. The lawmaker took the opportunity to ask him his reasons for refusing to cooperate with my endeavor and pleaded with him to change his attitude.

*   *   *

In any direct contact with the observed population, the researcher perhaps enters the field under the aegis of an official agency or as a social scientist directly identifying himself as such. In the present research, I took the second alternative. Any official sponsorship could have created serious difficulties because of the conflict existing among the members of the community, as well as their hostile attitude toward the government.

During the process of data gathering as a participant observer, I became a temporary member of the community without identifying with any of the political groups, thus avoiding a dual identity. I visited three to five families per day; I spent the rest of the day talking with shepherds and workers in the fields or taking notes. I conducted the interviews in Quechua in order to make the people feel comfortable and to facilitate a better and more precise expression of their feelings, opinions, attitudes, and ideas. I would always start conversations with flattering statements to elicit a discussion or a friendly argument. For example, I would approach a shepherd girl or a woman on her land by saying "you have such a large herd," or "you look beautiful on your plot," to which they would always answer by telling stories of their past or by comparing their land possession to that of some families whom they thought had more land than they needed.

Sometimes people would avoid the question and ask the reason for my stay in the area. I would tell women that I was in "search of a girl to marry," and this led to questions of their marital status, number of children, size of land, and so forth. Male peasants like conversations involving women, so I would approach them by asking whether there was any "available girl in the community, for everyone says that they are all yours; why do you not leave one for a poor guy like myself?" Some would name the single women or just smile at me. Others would bounce the question and say, "Why would you want another woman when you already have your blonde widow?" This approach worked much better than just knocking on doors with a long questionnaire in hand and saying: "Hi, I am doing research on peasant economy and would like you to answer some questions."

The purpose of the research had been to study the effects of land reform and modernization in the peasant community of Paras. A basic questionnaire designed to obtain data on the demographic, social, and economic aspects of the community was taken to the field. In the process of my visits and interviews I discovered that, right after the harvest, some peasants started making preparations for a long trip. Thus, my plan had to be changed. It needed to fit what was going in the field, which was different from what I had expected. After discovering the new research material, I centered my efforts on the *mantanero* peasants and some informants in small towns in the area. The reason informal conversations with indirect questions were formulated was that peasants are very sensitive to direct questions about themselves.

After defending my dissertation, I spent most of the summer of 1983 in Peru. The purposes of the trip were to study more closely the peasants of Paras who were connected to the underground economy, to make some exploratory visits to coca- and cocaine-producing communities, and to try to meet and become acquainted with experts in the industry.

My trip to the drug-plagued communities made many people think that I was a *pichicatero* (drug trafficker). On more than one occasion they offered me certain amounts of the "best stuff," but I cautiously avoided both too much information and direct or indirect involvement in drug trafficking. My cautious attitude owed to my suspicion that a trap had been set by local drug lords, many of whom had been my grade-school friends, high-school classmates, and fellow factory workers in Lima. Although to the people in the Andes I was continuing to do research on the changes in traditional communities, some suspected I was interested in something else. However, to them, that "something else" was not research but "white business."

My aluminum camera case was always the first thing to be searched at every police checkpoint. In many communities people thought that I was a foreigner. They whispered to each other in Quechua, saying "God knows what this *Colombiano* carries in that shiny case." Situations like this were opportunities to start conversations about drug production and traffic. Socializing with people at every level was my basic method of research. The disadvantage of this strategy is that it is time-consuming and limited to researchers with a deep knowledge of native language and culture.

*   *   *

On a bus I met two migrant workers from a village near my hometown who were coming back from the Upper Huallaga. They supplied the first details I had obtained on the preparation of coca paste. Three peasants from Paras not only provided the names and exact locations of research settings but also were willing to go with me to the jungles. A local teacher from a highland village who was taking a leave of absence to work on the coca plantations also became part of my direct connections to the underworld.

I traveled north to the hamlet where my friend the teacher was working. All I had were the names of the teacher's relatives, the nearby village, and a piece of paper giving vague directions. Despite the fact that I had asked the driver and his helper to drop me at the place where I had been told to get off, I missed my stop by about two kilometers. I got off at a place where about ten people were picking coca leaves, and I walked back until I found the right house. Neither my friend the teacher nor his relatives were home. The man in charge of the small hardware store was very apathetic toward me. When I asked him about the owner of the house, he brusquely answered, "He is not in."

My hosts introduced me to the area residents as one of their relatives from Lima visiting them for a few weeks. I spent the first days of fieldwork socializing. As days passed, I got deeper and deeper into the underground economy and subculture, avoiding direct questions regarding formulas, proportions, procedures, and prices. I participated in every routine or special event I could and observed others. For example, after a volleyball game among local residents, I sat and had refreshments with the neighbors who usually asked about my plans for the next day. I was always open to suggestions and invitations to visit their plantations or their farmhouses deep in the forests. Often, the trips involved hours of hiking, especially when the visits were to secret airfields.

Following a successful stay, I would move to other sites. The strategy was always to produce networks of friendship. But I never went anywhere without actually knowing the setting and the host families. This meant many hours of traveling, by car, bus, truck, or on foot. My peasant friends from Paras helped me cross passes and mountain ranges to reach areas that did not have road service. They always made jokes about my limited physical endurance. For the longer hikes, my traveling equipment consisted of my worn-out sleeping bag, a small tin pot in which to boil water, some matches, basic medicines, my 35-milimeter camera, and many rolls of film. Hunger and thirst made us drop in on communities or isolated houses during the treks across the mountain ranges. Under the pretext of having the peasant women cook our meals, we stopped overnight in houses and huts where friends or acquaintances of my peasant hiking experts lived. Questions such as "What brings you here?" and "Where are you from?" were constantly addressed to me. To them, I was from Llamellín, my hometown. Some peasants, especially males, tested me with their questions. My responses never failed to reassure them about my identity.

The actual recording of data varied according to the conditions in the settings, types of subjects, and kinds of information needed. Days in the highlands are short and the majority of people do not have electricity. Wax candles, kerosene lanterns, and flashlights are used by those who can afford them. I therefore made field notes immediately following interviews and conversations during the day. Evenings and nights were usually spent chatting with neighbors in my village of residence. Thus, the apparent physical disadvantage of the setting turned into an advantage. Evening and night conversations and discussions were ways to double-check information I had collected.

I gathered data on coca-leaf economy, costs and process of manufacturing, and national and international trafficking of coca paste and cocaine at different places in the country. Knowledge of every aspect of the underground hustle and bustle came from direct observation and participation. As I had good rapport with the people, some days I would ask them to let me drop in to their work settings. Then I would show up with a couple of bottles of beer, Coca-Cola, or anything that would season my visit. During the first visits, I tried not to be too inquisitive, for I perceived tension in some individuals, especially the full-time cocaine entrepreneurs. As had happened in the highlands in 1980, patience and good humor paid good returns.

*   *   *

The study, besides being an intellectual and an academic endeavor, was an opportunity for photographic expression. If my two native tongues, Quechua and Spanish, were extremely valuable during data collection, my photographic skills were equally important. Since my first visits to my hometown in the mid-1970s, I have been photographing the people and the culture of the Andes. Hundreds of exposures of color slides document my presence and knowledge of the Andean countries at large. The visual side of the research in and of itself represents a whole new dimension of social research. However, a camera hanging on the researcher's neck can be potentially dangerous when people do not want to be photographed and sometimes brought me rejection, disappointment, and setbacks.

In 1973, during my first visit to my hometown from New York, I wanted to photograph the people from a nearby village. I found two peasant shepherd boys who seemed to make an interesting picture. I aimed my camera mounted with a long telephoto lens. One of the children realized that I was snapping the camera. The boys started screaming and throwing stones at me. A few minutes later, parents and neighbors came out with their dogs, sticks, and more stones. They thought that I had been trying to shoot the children with a gun. On another occasion during fieldwork in 1981, a peasant asked me to use my camera to see whether there was underground water in the mountains surrounding the community.

If in the Andes my nightly research companion was a cassette recorder, during the day my camera was the research associate always hanging on my shoulder, ready to freeze segments and instants of what was happening in the community. However, photographing and taping subjects raises the ethical question of whether or not the participants in the research should be made aware of the use of audiovisual devices during research contact. Many Andean populations are sensitive to having their voices taped or their images recorded on film. The experiences noted earlier made me more cautious in the taping and photographing I did afterwards.

Strangers carrying cameras are not yet seen in the cocaine towns and villages, because there is no such thing as tourists or visitors taking snapshots of farms and landscapes or posing with natives for a souvenir photo. In the underground world, nobody wants to be photographed regardless of his status. Obviously, not everyone toting a camera is a journalist. On the other hand, there is no way for the illegal world to know whether an occasional visitor is a drug spy or an undercover law-enforcement agent. They suspect that anyone taking pictures of them working is an enemy. This may be one of the reasons why photographs or films that reach our attention have almost always been taken under police protection or as part of a crackdown or a drug bust. These kinds of photographs and films are more sensational and biased. Lack of respect and consideration for the subject breaks the interrelationship between the photographer and his subject. Furthermore, the police seem to be oriented toward showing how excellent the control and eradication programs are or publicizing widespread drug abuse.

On the last day of my stay in the green mines, I decided to take some pictures of a busy Sunday in one of the cocaine centers. When a peasant friend and I were walking around the main square taking candid shots of migrant workers, three men approached us. They pointed at me and said, "You are an outsider, aren't you?" Then they asked whether my cameras were for sale. I replied no. They all deliberated briefly. They asked me at which hotel I was staying. I gave the name of a low-class hotel. Their advice was that I should leave town immediately. They showed me the park bench where two reporters had been shot to death a few feet from where I was standing and emphasized their advice by saying,

"If you don't pack and leave the town immediately you'll be another statistic; so if you want to live longer than twenty-four hours, get the hell out of here."

I thanked them for their advice and expressed my gratitude for their concern. I accepted the glass of beer they invited me to drink. Isn't life full of hellos and good-byes? What had happened to me in the highlands in 1980 was repeated at the other end of my research. This time, however, rather than trying to make friends as I had done in the highlands, I put my gear away, walked around the square, and left the town.

Photo courtesy of Edmundo Morales.

Photo courtesy of Edmundo Morales.

Laud Humphreys

The Sociologist as Voyeur

One of the most controversial studies in the history of sociology was conducted by the late Laud Humphreys in the 1960s. Taking the role of "watchqueen" or lookout, Humphreys observed the interactions between homosexual men seeking casual sexual encounters in public restrooms ("tearooms"). When he published his findings in Tearoom Trade: Impersonal Sex in Public Places, *Humphreys was criticized by many of his colleagues for invading the men's privacy. (Others defended him for daring to investigate a taboo subject, noting that he had been careful to keep the men's identities secret.)*

Humphreys, a priest turned sociologist, began his studies of homosexual behavior in an effort to understand the problems of homosexual parishioners who came to him for counseling. Unlike previous researchers, he decided to focus on men who were outside the gay subculture, who participated in the gay world only to the extent of satisfying their sexual needs. In other words, he carried out a study of a group of people engaging in deviant behavior for whom deviance was highly individual yet occurred within a specific social structure. He did not explore why they engaged in that behavior or the role it played in their personal lives; he studied the behavior itself—oral sex between adult males in public rest-

This selection is adapted with permission from Laud Humphreys, *Tearoom Trade: Impersonal Sex in Public Places* (New York: Aldine de Gruyter). Copyright © 1970, 1975 by R. A. Laud Humphreys.

rooms—and attempted to identify the unspoken rules that guided that behavior.

In this selection Humphreys describes how he developed his research method and learned how to pass as deviant. He frankly addresses the ethical issues involved in this form of participant observation. He also notes some of the complexities of this research approach. For example, suspicion: "Any man who remains in a public washroom for more than five minutes is apt to be either a member of the vice squad or someone on the make." Another complication, not mentioned in this selection, is the attitude of law enforcement agents; on one occasion Humphreys allowed himself to be jailed rather than alert the police to the nature of his research.

In 1975 the second edition of Tearoom Trade *was published. It included a "Retrospect" in which Humphreys commented on the controversy that had erupted when the first edition appeared. His closing remarks provide a poignant glimpse of the researcher's feelings for the people he had observed:*

Years have passed since I studied the tearoom encounters and those who enact a hidden portion of their lives in them. There is no reason to believe that any research subjects have suffered because of my efforts . . . At the same time, I realize that serving as a focus for ethical debate is no mean contribution. Above all, I know that this study is increasingly cited by attorneys seeking acquittal for clients arrested in public restrooms. What began as a relatively uncomplicated ethnography of the gay community . . . ended as much in a quest for justice as for knowledge alone. (pp. 231–32).

In the summer of 1965, I wrote a research paper on the subject of homosexuality. After reading the paper, my graduate adviser raised a question, the answer to which was not available from my data or from the literature on sexual deviance: "But where does the average guy go just to get a blow job? That's where you should do your research." I suspected that the answer was "to the tearooms," but this was little more than a hunch. We decided that this area of covert deviant behavior, tangential to the subculture, was one that needed study.

Stories of tearoom adventures and raids constantly pass along the homosexual grapevine. There is a great deal of talk (usually of a pejorative nature) about these facilities in gay circles. Most men with whom I had conversed at any length during my brief research admitted to "tricking" (engaging in one-time sexual relationships) in tearooms from time to time.

Sociologists had studied bar operations and the practice of male prostitution by teenage gang members, but no one had tackled the scenes of impersonal sex where most arrests are made. Literature on the subject indicates that, up to now, the police and other law enforcement agents have been the only systematic observers of homosexual action in public restrooms. Social scientists have avoided this area of deviant behavior, perhaps due to the many emotional and methodological problems it presents—some of which are common to any study of a deviant population. The obstructions encountered in the course of this study—insurmountable as some appeared at the time—are, for the most part, shared with other ethnographers, particularly those who take on deviant populations.

Unless one intends to study only that beleaguered, captive population, the students in our college classrooms, the first problem is one of locating subjects for research. My initial problem was one of locating the more popular tearooms. Once I could find where the "action" was, I knew that potential research subjects would be involved. This is the advantage of studying a population defined only by their participation in a specific sort of interaction. Mine was not a study of "homosexuals" but of participants in homosexual acts. The subjects of this study have but one thing in common: Each has been observed by me in the course of a homosexual act in a public park restroom. This is the activity, and these are the actors, that I set out to study in 1965.

When a researcher is able to engage participants in conversation outside the tearooms, he may be directed to some of the more active spots of a city. In the early stages of research, however, such measures as location, surroundings, and the number of cars parked in front are very helpful in locating the more profitable places for research. My study has been focused upon park facilities for two reasons. First, the latter have the greatest notoriety in the homosexual subculture. Second, I wanted to control the ecological and demographic variables as much as possible. All but two of the restrooms in which I conducted systematic observations were of the same floor plan, and all shared common environmental conditions. Of greater importance is the "democratic" nature of outdoor facilities. Parks are much more apt to draw a representative sample of the population.

In the same city, there is a well-known tearoom in a courthouse, another in a large department store, and a third in the basement of a class B movie theater. Each caters to a different clientele, is subject to different influences from the physical surroundings, and is supervised by different forces of social control. In the department store tearoom, most of the men wear neckties. Participants venture there during lunch hour from their nearby offices. This is a white-collar facility, patrolled by the store's detectives. Word has it that an apprehended offender is taken to the office of the store manager, who administers reprimands and threats and then pronounces sentence: He revokes the guilty man's credit card! I once spent an hour counseling a distraught participant who was contemplating suicide in apprehension of what his wife might be told if she tried to charge anything at this popular store, where her husband had been caught in an act of fellatio.

Although I have made informal observations of tearoom activity in New York, Chicago, St. Louis, Kansas City, Des Moines, Tulsa, Denver, Los Angeles, and San Francisco, the greater part of the research was concentrated in one metropolitan area. Variables such as climate, availability of parks, the nature of police surveillance, amount of newspaper publicity accorded offenders, or relative popularity of other sexual outlets could result in wide variations in the volume of tearoom activity. My contention, however, is that the basic rules of the game—and the profile of the players—are applicable to any place in the United States.

This much may be said with certainty: There is probably no major city in the nation without its tearooms in current operation. These facilities constitute a major part of the free sex market for those in the homosexual subculture—and for millions who might never identify with the gay society. For the social scientist, these public toilets provide a means for direct observation of the dynamics of sexual encounters *in situ;* moreover, they facilitate the gathering of a representative sample of secret deviants, for most of whom association with the deviant subculture is minimal.

I employed the methods described herein not because they are the most accurate in the sense of "neatness" or "cleanness" but because they promised the greatest accuracy in terms of faithfulness to people and actions as they live and happen. These are strategies that I judged to be the least obtrusive measures available—the least likely to distort the real world.

Some methods have grown quite naturally from the chromosomal messages of a particular "school" of sociology. Others are mutations resulting from interaction with my research environment. As obstacles developed, means were devised to circumvent them. Unusual difficulties call for unusual strategies.

My concern in this study has been with the description of a specific style of deviant behavior and of the population who engage in that activity. I have not attempted to test any prestated hypotheses. Such an approach tends to limit sociological research to the imagery of the physical sciences. It seems to me equally valid to apply a number of measures to one population or one type of social interaction for the purpose of describing that encounter and its participants. Hypotheses should develop *out of* such ethnographic work, rather than provide restrictions and distortions from its inception.

The research in which I engaged, from the summer of 1965 through the winter of 1967-68, may be broken down into two distinct stages, each with its subcategories. The first was an ethnographic or participant-observation stage. This part of the research extended over two years on a part-time basis (I was also involved in graduate study at the time).

The second half involved six months of full-time work in administering interview schedules to more than 100 respondents and in attempting to interview another twenty-seven. Another year was devoted to analysis of the resulting data.

As an ethnographer, my first task was to acquaint myself with the homosexual subculture. Because of my pastoral experience, I was not a total stranger to those circles. While a seminarian, I was employed for two years in a parish that was known in the homosexual world as Chicago's "queen parish"—a place to which the homosexuals could turn for counsel, understanding priests, good music, and worship with an aesthetic emphasis. I soon came to know the gay parisioners and to speak their language. Seminarians who worked there called on people who lived in unbelievable squalor and in houses of prostitution, so it was nothing for us to seek the flock in gay bars as well. One of the faithful churchmen was bartender and part-time entertainer in one of the more popular spots, and he always looked after the seminarians and warned us of impending raids.

From 1955 to 1965, I served parishes in Oklahoma, Colorado, and Kansas, twice serving as Episcopal campus chaplain on a part-time basis. Because I was considered "wise" and did not attempt to "reform" them, hundreds of homosexuals of all sorts and conditions came to me during those years for counseling.

The problem, at the beginning of my research, was threefold: to become acquainted with the sociological literature on sexual deviance; to gain entry to a deviant subculture in a strange city where I no longer had pastoral, and only part-time priestly, duties; and to begin to listen to sexual deviants with a scientist's rather than a pastor's ear.

Like any deviant group, homosexuals have developed defenses against outsiders: secrecy about their true identity, symbolic gestures and the use of the eyes for communication, unwillingness to expose the whereabouts of their meeting places, extraordinary caution with strangers, and admission to certain places only in the company of a recognized person. Shorn of pastoral contacts and unwilling to use professional credentials, I had to enter the subculture as would any newcomer and to make contact with respondents under the guise of being another gay guy.

Such entry is not difficult to accomplish. Almost any taxi driver can tell a customer where to find a gay bar. A guide to such gathering places may be purchased for $5.00. The real problem is not one of making contact with the subculture but of making the contact "stick." Acceptance does not come easy, and it is extremely difficult to move beyond superficial contact in public places to acceptance by the group and invitations to private and semiprivate parties.

On one occasion, for instance, tickets to an after-hours party were sold to the man next to me at a bar. When I asked to buy one, I was told that they were "full up." Following the tip of another customer, I showed up anyway and walked right in. No one questioned my being there. Since my purpose at this point of the field study was simply to "get the feel" of the deviant community rather than to study methods of penetrating its boundaries, I finally tired of the long method and told a friendly potential respondent who I was and what I was doing. He then got me invited to cocktail parties before the annual "drag ball," and my survey of the subculture neared completion.

During those first months, I made the rounds of ten gay bars then operating in the metropolitan area, attended private gatherings and the annual ball, covered the scene where male prostitutes operate out of a coffee house, observed pick-up operations in the parks and streets, and had dozens of informal interviews with participants in the gay society. I also visited the locales where "instant sex" was to be had: the local bathhouse, certain movie theaters, and the tearooms.

From the beginning, my decision was to continue the practice of the field study in passing as deviant. Although this raises questions of scientific ethics, there are good reasons for following this method of participant observation.

In the first place, I am convinced that there is only *one* way to watch highly discreditable behavior and that is to pretend to be in the same boat with those engaging in it. To wear a button that says "I Am a Watchbird, Watching You" into a tearoom, would instantly eliminate all action except the flushing of toilets and the exiting of all present.

The second reason is to prevent distortion. Hypothetically, let us assume that a few men could be found to continue their sexual activity while under observation. How "normal" could that activity be? How could the researcher separate the "show" and the "cover" from standard procedures of the encounter? Masters and Johnson might gather clinical data in a clinical setting without distortion, but a stage is a suitable research site only for those who wish to study the "onstage" behavior of actors.

Observation is made doubly difficult when the observer is an object of suspicion. Any man who remains in a public washroom for more than five minutes is apt to be either a member of the vice squad or someone on the make. As yet, he is not suspected as being a social scientist. The researcher, concerned as he is in uncovering information, is unavoidably at variance with the secretive interests of the deviant population. Because his behavior is both criminal and the object of much social derision, the tearoom customer is exceptionally sensitive to the intrusion of all strangers.

When the focus of an encounter is specifically sexual, it is very difficult for the observer to take a "natural part" in the action without actual involvement of a sexual nature. Such involvement would, of course, raise serious questions of both scientific and ethical integrity on his part. His central problem, then, is one of maintaining both objectivity and participation.

My preliminary observations of tearoom encounters led to the discovery of an essential strategy—the real methodological breakthrough of this research. The very fear and suspicion encountered in the restrooms produces a participant role, the sexuality of which is optional. This is the role of the lookout ("watchqueen" in the argot), a man who is situated at the door or windows from which he may observe the means of access to the restroom. When someone approaches, he coughs. He nods when the coast is clear or if he recognizes an entering party as a regular.

The lookouts fall into three main types. The most common of these are the "waiters," men who are waiting for someone with whom they have made an appointment or whom they expect to find at this spot, for a particular type of "trick," or for a chance to get in on the action. The others are the masturbaters, who engage in autoerotic behavior (either overtly or beneath their clothing) while observing sexual acts, and the voyeurs, who appear to derive sexual stimulation and pleasure from watching the others. Waiters sometimes masturbate while waiting—and I have no evidence to prove some are not also voyeurs. The point is that the primary purpose of their presence differs from that of the pure masturbater or voyeur: The waiters expect to become players. In a sense, the masturbaters are all voyeurs, while the reverse is not true.

In terms of appearances, I assumed the role of the voyeur—a role superbly suited for sociologists and the only lookout role that is not overtly sexual. On those occasions when there was only one other man present in the room, I have taken a role that is even less sexual than that of the voyeur-lookout: the straight person who has come to the facility for purposes of elimination. Although it avoids sexual pressure, this role is problematic for the researcher: It is short-lived and invariably disrupts the action he has set out to observe.

Before being alerted to the role of lookout by a cooperating respondent, I tried first the role of the straight and then that of the waiter. As the former, I disrupted the action and frustrated my research. As the latter—glancing at my watch and pacing nervously from window to door to peer out—I could not stay long without being invited to enter the action and could only make furtive observation of the encounters. As it was, the waiter and voyeur roles are subject to blurring and I was often mistaken for the former.

By serving as a voyeur-lookout, I was able to move around the room at will, from window to window, and to observe all that went on without alarming my respondents or otherwise disturbing the action. I found this role much more amenable and profitable than the limited roles assumed in the earlier stages of research.

Charles Bosk

The Fieldworker and the Surgeon

For eighteen months Charles Bosk was a participant observer in the surgical training program at a large teaching hospital. His research was designed to explore three themes: social control (how does the medical profession evaluate and control the behavior of its members?); social support (how do physicians control the performance of subordinates yet allow them room to make honest errors?); and dealing with failure (how do surgeons cope with the knowledge that their errors sometimes cause suffering and death?).

"Pacific Hospital," where Bosk conducted his research, is an elite teaching institution surrounded by a lower-class neighborhood whose residents often seek medical care at the hospital's emergency room. The surgical staff at Pacific Hospital must treat many patients who are in extreme pain, often as a result of traumas such as gunshot wounds or stabbings. Thus, the surgeons must often work under conditions that are far from ideal, making errors more likely.

Bosk was permitted to observe the operations of two surgical services, focusing on the ways in which errors are detected, evaluated, and corrected. He followed surgeons through their daily activities: visiting pa-

Parts of this selection are adapted from Charles Bosk, *Forgive and Remember: Managing Medical Failure.* © 1979 by The University of Chicago. Abridgment © 1989 by The University of Chicago. All rights reserved. Adapted with permission of The University of Chicago Press. The last part of this selection is from "The Fieldworker as Watcher and Witness," *Hastings Center Report* 15, no. 3. (Hastings-on-Hudson, N.Y.: Society of Ethics and Life Sciences, June 1985).

tients twice daily on rounds; drinking coffee in the doctors' lounge during time-out periods; assisting on operations when hands were short; standing by when bodies were pronounced dead; staying on call at night. He became aware of the shared world view of the members of the surgical work group, the way they judge themselves and others, and their attitudes toward patients. He found that resident surgeons are forgiven if they make mistakes that the older surgeons believe to be "normal" aspects of the learning process. They are not forgiven, however, when their mistakes are repeated or are throught to be due to carelessness.

In this selection Bosk describes many of the issues that must be confronted by researchers working in delicate situations in which confidentiality is absolutely essential.

As I reflect on the experience of eighteen months of participant observation in a teaching hospital, and on the dilemmas of the observer role, I feel a sense of respect for data-collecting procedures which allow the researcher to keep the sensuous world at a distance, and which thereby allow him to avoid the self-exposure, self-reflection, and self-doubt endemic to fieldworkers. In the field, the everyday life of his subjects overwhelms the researcher, threatens to obliterate his sense of self, and forces a reconsideration of deeply held personal and intellectual beliefs. It would be of little point, then, for me to pretend that I was merely a coding machine which transcribed the events of everyday life into field material. Instead, I would like to describe the field experience itself.

How did I begin? The first thing I did was to approach an attending [physician] I had met at a party, explain my proposed study, and ask for his cooperation. The attending expressed enthusiasm for the project, but refused his cooperation. He claimed that if I wanted to really be trusted, I would need the housestaff's acceptance. He expressed his fear that his sponsorship would be a "kiss of death": Housestaff would view me as his spy and never talk freely with me. If I wanted my project to succeed, he advised, I needed to be seen as my own person. So rather than somehow magically start the research, he gave me the names of a number of residents.

Not sure if I was receiving aid or a runaround from my initial contact, I called the first name on his list, the chief resident. We met for coffee and I explained my plans. The resident approved my being an observer on his service, but claimed he would have to check with both attendings. The chairman of my department provided a letter of introduction to the chairman of the Department of Surgery. Gaining my initial entree was a multistaged diplomatic problem. Each interaction was a test, and access was the result of continual testing and retesting. Entree was not something negotiated once and then over and done with.

Access—being allowed in the scene—is one thing, but approval and trust of field subjects is quite another. Much is made in fieldwork accounts of the "cover story" which the observer uses to explain his presence in the setting as a first and essential step in gaining trust. My cover story was very simple. I explained that I was doing a dissertation on the way surgeons learned to recognize and control error. The surgeons were, as a rule, remarkably uncurious about my research. None ever questioned the legitimacy of my research question or the nature of my methods during our initial meetings. Few even requested that I account for my presence. I was not asked for my cover story very often and, when asked for the story, I was not required to elaborate on it. In some sense, my access was secured by sponsorship of housestaff trusted by all. Once my access was established, my cover story was superfluous.

Trust was gained neither during initial introductions nor by the artful manipulation of a cover story, but through my performance in roles I assumed and was assigned by housestaff and attendings. Housestaff assigned me a number of roles. Most generally, I was an "extra pair of hands" and a "gofer." During the time of my fieldwork, I became very proficient at opening packages of bandages, retrieving charts, and fetching items from the supply room. Through these tasks, I expressed some solidarity with whatever group I was observing and gave something, however inconsequential, in exchange for "observing rights."

Second, I was an "emissary from the outside world." My round of life was less circumscribed than a houseofficer's: I read and watched more news, saw more movies, and participated more fully in university life outside the hospital. In some sense, I provided housestaff contact with a world they felt cut off from. During Watergate, I always brought a number of papers into the hospital. How or why this became my task I do not know. Often I purchased these papers at the hospital gift stand, a place interns and residents certainly had access to. Their general reluctance to pick such papers up is not so much a mark of their frugality as a symbolic statement about their relation to the world outside Pacific Hospital. I later learned that housestaff attach a magical property to newspapers, books, and magazines. If they bring them in to work they see this as jinxing themselves and condemning the group to an impossible, busy day. It is, however, permissible for outsiders to bring such taboo items to them. My passing remarks about movies, current events, the weather—all were taken as an indication of what educated people on the outside were thinking.

Third, I was a "fellow-sufferer." As a graduate student not released from training, I was perceived as occupying a position analogous to the houseofficer's. My own career problems and expectations were topics that houseofficers initiated much conversation about. They constantly compared and contrasted our different experiences. During such exchanges, houseofficers constantly emphasized the indignity of their roles and often suggested that their present burdens justified their future rewards. From me, they sought to learn about the generalized indignities of the subordinate role in sociological training. I regaled them with my wildest recollections of coding data and proofreading galleys.

Fourth, I was a convenient "sounding board." I was surprised at the degree that informants sought me out to relate stories of practice that they disagreed with. Feelings that were not shared in the group, discontents, uncertainties were taken to me. I knew that observers were often sought by organizational malcontents; what surprised me was that all my informants were at one time or another malcontents. Disfiguring palliative operations, patient discomfort, and the openness of communications among the ranks were the most common complaints. As a "sounding board," I was implicitly asked to play a quasi-therapeutic role: to listen without judging and to understand.

Fifth, houseofficers viewed me as a "referee" in conflicts among themselves over patient management, quarrels over the equity of the division of labor, and disputes about whether or not patients understood what was happening. In the midst of such disagreements, one houseofficer would turn to me and ask: "Well, what do you think? Which of us is right?" These were not comfortable situations for me when I could hide behind the observer role. A judgment was demanded as the price for my continued presence. Moreover, any judgment was certain to alienate one of my informants. I developed tactics for throwing the question back to the disputants or for pointing out the merits of either side, or making a joke of the entire dispute. Over time, I tried in vain to teach my subjects that such conflict resolution was not a proper part of my role. Nevertheless, being asked to referee disputes was a recurrent and always problematic task and not one that I ever felt totally comfortable with. As I felt more accepted, I was somewhat better able to put questions off. But in the beginning, I was stiff, uncomfortable, and always mindful of my relationships with each party.

Sixth, I was the group "historian." Because of the way housestaff rotate through the various services, it was not unusual for me to have been on a given service longer than any particular houseofficer. When this occurred, I was expected to know something of the history of the different patients on the service. I was expected to keep track of attendings' remarks and verify them for absent group members. The role of group historian served me well, since it forced housestaff to depend on me for information that they needed. This created a greater sense of mutual obligation between housestaff and myself and to the degree that the information I supplied was reliable, I established my credibility. Also, I was a short-run as well as long-run historian. I would often ask housestaff about action that I could not watch but was interested in. On more than one occasion, my questioning reminded houseofficers of a task that had until then slipped their minds. My unwitting reminders saved them from oversights which would have gotten them into trouble. The fact that such incidents occurred further indebted housestaff to me and heightened my legitimacy. A fieldworker pays a price for this kind of legitimacy, though. The historian role itself presents some of the most common moral dilemmas that a field-worker faces. Each time I gave such a reminder to a houseofficer, I changed what would have otherwise happened without this intervention. Lab tests, consultations with other physicians, and conferences with patients and their families—all these were on occasion events that took place because I reminded houseofficers of them. By jogging the memory of houseofficers in this way, I made it impossible for myself to observe what happens when these events fail to occur.

Despite the fact that it was not my intention in these instances to change the action I was studying, one can see very clearly that errors of omission present the observer with a moral dilemma. If one does remind a houseofficer, one disturbs by that act the very relationships one is attempting to study. However, if one does not remind the houseofficer—and yet knows he has overlooked something—it is possible that a patient's care will be compromised. In most cases when I asked if something had been done, I did so because as a sociologist I was particularly interested in seeing or hearing a report of that specific action, and usually because I was unaware of whether it had occurred or not—I was trying to orient myself. If the houseofficer had forgotten about the task I was asking about, if it had completely slipped his mind, then that fact told me something about the difference between a sociological perspective and a surgical one; and I learned something more about the structure of the surgeon's life-world.

If errors of omission present observers with one type of moral dilemma, errors of commission present him with another. In the case where the fieldworker knows that some harm has been done to a patient through physician or nursing error, does the observer have any direct, ethical obligations to the patient and his/her family? That is, should the fieldworker either inform the patient or find some alternative means of making public the error? I chose not to do this for a variety of reasons. As a pragmatic matter, being a patient-advocate would have made the kind of fieldwork I wanted to do impossible. Moreover, I felt a responsibility to other medical sociologists who wished to undertake field projects in the future. I was aware that my conduct could either make the way more or less difficult for those who followed me. While some participant-observer effects seem acceptable to me, others, those that contravene the basic operating norms of a group, are not acceptable. These larger effects not only distort the phenomenon under study, they make it impossible for later fieldworkers to gain access to and legitimacy within medical settings. Most important, I felt I could discharge my ethical obligations to patients more effectively by describing the general categorization and management of error rather than tilting at windmills in one or two select cases.

Whatever roles houseofficers cast me in or I assumed, the major irony of the fieldworker role was always apparent: On the one hand, I was intimately involved in all aspects of the everyday life of a group; and on the other hand, I was constrained by the nature of my task to exert as little social influence in that group as possible. So, my sensitivity to the group's actions and their consequences was heightened at the same time that my theoretic commitments restrained me from even raising the group's consciousness about the effects of its own actions.

I had less intimate contact with attendings than with housestaff, and assumed and was assigned a narrower range of roles. Most commonly, I was seen as any other "medical student." Attendings assimilated me to the group by treating me like any other member of the group. They had me look down proctoscopy tubes, rake abdomens feeling for a mass, and learn to hold retractors properly. Their treatment of me helped strengthen my ties to houseofficers, who saw that not only was I not in league with attendings, but that, like them, I was the occasional butt of an attending's sense of humor. By the same token, my own willingness to take part this way in group life served notice to attendings that I was willing to do what was necessary to complete my project. When attendings viewed me as a medical student, they often tried to teach me concise medical lessons. Whatever problems of identification and rapport I might have had, it is interesting to note that attendings had some of their own. Toward the end of my fieldwork, two attendings approached me, told me that I must be interested in medicine to have spent so much time at Pacific Hospital, and then informed me that if I wanted to go to medical school, they would help me in any way they could. I took their offer as an indication that perhaps I had been in the field long enough.

The incident above is related to another role attendings cast me in—their "advisee." Attendings offered two types of advice. First, there was "scientific" advice. Here attendings would address themselves to the design of my study. They wanted to know about my control groups, my measurement instruments, my hypotheses, and all similar paraphernalia from the type of research they engaged in. When I would explain that my model for research was somewhat different from theirs, they were skeptical but generally tolerant. After all, I was the sociology department's problem, and not theirs. Second, attendings offered "interpretive advice." When we were alone, they would often explain why they acted in certain situations the way they did, what they felt to be the burdens of their authority, what the major problems doing surgery in a major medical center were, what the personal strengths and weaknesses of their colleagues were, and so on.

In addition, attendings used me often as a "clown" to diffuse tensions in the group. When things were going poorly, attendings on occasion would question me like any other member of the group and then poke fun at my fumbling and ignorance. Sitting around the doctors' lounge, the rigors of academic life would be compared unfavorably with those of surgery; and my manly virtues would be impugned. It was not always as a clown that attendings used me to ease tensions. Just as with housestaff, I was asked to referee conflict. My study was used by them to deflect conversations from their course. So that often when faced with troublesome questions from nurses or other physicians, they would give a noncommittal response and then ask me to explain my study. They would ply me with questions until they were sure the conversation could safely resume.

*   *   *

The problem of objective description and analysis is in itself formidable. In fieldwork, the problem is made more complex because of the deep relationships and attachments one builds over time to one's subjects. As Charles Lidz[1] has correctly pointed out, the right and privilege of being an observer is a gift presented to the researcher by his host and subjects. I would agree with Lidz that the recognition and proper understanding of the gift relationship serves as both a convenient theoretical framework for understanding the peculiar dilemmas of the fieldworker and at the same time a formidable restraint on bias in observation and interpretation.

The giver and the recipient of a gift are involved in an interactional sequence that involves giving, receiving, and reciprocating. Even more important, involvement in a gift cycle creates a solidarity among participants and signifies that they have obligations toward each other that extend into the future. The fact that the fieldworker is both the receiver of a gift and a guest means that he has a diffuse sense of obligation to his host-giver-subject. Fieldworkers have long recognized their indebtedness to their subjects. While not explicitly analyzing the observer role as a gift relationship, fieldworkers worry over fulfilling their obligations to their subjects, over balancing personal debts to individuals against universal debts to the discipline of sociology, and over discharging obligations to subjects that extend beyond the life of any particular piece of research. In addition, there is the fieldworker's typical ethical dilemma: What if the data I gather are potentially harmful to my subjects? What if the facts themselves betray those to whom I have become so attached over so many months? Others have spoken of the "tyranny of the gift" in different contexts, but it is clear that the gift of access, of witnessing social life as it is lived in someone else's environment, exercises a tyranny of its own. This tyranny has as its most distinctive features three significant elements: (1) the danger of overrapport, so thoroughly merging with the subject's point of view that one cannot achieve the critical distance necessary for analysis; (2) the danger of overindebtedness, so thoroughly feeling a sense of diffuse obligation that one can no longer assess what one does and does not properly owe his subjects; and (3) the danger of overgeneralization, so thoroughly idealizing one's subjects that one sees their behavior as overly representative of all persons in a class.

I was protected from overrapport and overindebtedness in part by the very structure of hospital life. Unlike fieldworkers who spend years with an unchanging population, my subjects rotated through the surgical services fairly rapidly. Some stayed for as little as a month; none stayed over three months. There were housestaff I liked very much; housestaff I detested; and others I barely got to know. Whatever the case, there was an unending parade of housestaff. The mere fact that I was observing so many people in rapid succession prevented overrapport with any one subject.

My resolution to the problem of overindebtedness was somewhat different from the resolution of the problem of overrapport. A moderately sensitive observer of life in the surgery wards of a hospital will be flooded with feelings of helplessness. These feelings themselves have two distinct components. First, witnessing so much pain and suffering, the fieldworker wants to roll up his sleeves and do something, anything. At the same time, seeing death as an everyday event makes one guilty and overly aware of one's own good fortune. As a fieldworker, I was often made uncomfortable by what I saw. I felt I had stumbled into incredibly intimate and significant slices of patients' and doctors' lives. Much like any person who sees more than he would like of a friend's life, I felt guilty about some of the knowledge I had gained, worried over what the boundary between privileged information and data was, and wondered about how I repaid my obligation to my subjects. In the short run, the housestaff resolved the problem of helplessness and indebtedness by the roles they cast for me. When housestaff demanded that I help out by wheeling the chart rack, opening dressings, acting as a group memory, they provided me a means to cope with my own helplessness and assuage my guilt at the same time that they incorporated me into the group.

Overgeneralization is also a recurrent problem for fieldworkers. There is the danger that one particular event will become etched in the fieldworker's memory as emblematic of the way action is organized in an environment. That is to say, fieldworkers may overgeneralize incidents and see them as representative of categories of action. I avoided overgeneralization by making sure I had at least two independently generated examples of the same phenomenon before I began to make inferences.

My operating rule here was, as far as I can see, not fundamentally different from those that survey researchers use to ensure reliability in their studies. Also, I was very careful to follow particular incidents through many levels of social organization. For example, I was able to test my inferences about normative error in the promotion meeting, where I observed the criteria attending surgeons use to judge the fitness of housestaff for surgical careers. Throughout my fieldwork, I was very careful to test observations in one context against those of another.

On the other hand, there are observations I made that did not find their way into the fieldwork because I felt my inferential base was too thin. On one occasion I watched a series of unexpected deaths and complications, which occurred in quick succession, temporarily destroy the morale of one of the services I was observing. These occurred during the end of a rotation, while a chief resident was on vacation. I developed an explanation which related the occurrence of failure and group panic. However, during the rest of my fieldwork, I did not have the opportunity to observe another rash of failures. As a result, such speculations did not find their way into my published work.

*   *   *

When I was in the middle of the field, disguising the place and principals of my study was not as easy as it is in this report. I was always aware when I spoke that others knew those I spoke of, and that a too-loose tongue could hurt me and them in many untold ways. Since I promised my subjects confidentiality and anonymity, the "cover story" I devised to manage social situations was as consequential as the one I devised to manage field introductions. Only by assuring confidentiality and anonymity could I satisfy my subjects that my study would be within the bounds of current medical ethics. Both promises present some dilemmas, however.

First, I could never be sure that some enterprising person would not be able to figure out my place and principals. Essentially, confidentiality and anonymity were the promises I made but I had little control over their fulfillment. There have been recent debates about whether fieldworkers should go to the bother of making general "covering names" for their sites, and whether they should disguise their subjects. It seems to me that such fictitious names do more than provide confidentiality and anonymity: They highlight the generalized features of our descriptions and minimize the particularized aspects. To my mind, this aspect of naming is even more important in some ways than confidentiality and anonymity in that it creates a fieldwork literature rather than a description of specific places.

Others have advocated that to make fieldwork more rigorous and to display our methodology more openly, we should open our notebooks to the curious. Such procedure would allow others to see how we manipulate our data and fit the canons of science in general. Such a proposal troubles me because, as a sociologist, I gathered litigable material from subjects who trusted me. As a sociologist, I have no legal right to claim a privileged or confidential relationship with my subjects; my notes are subpoenable. If I opened my notebooks in the manner necessary to make clear the operations I performed on my data, I risk having those notebooks put to uses other than those I approve of. Involved here is a difficult problem: how to afford my subjects and myself enough protection so that we feel comfortable doing the study, at the same time displaying my data in a way that assures others of the validity and reliability of my research. I have indicated what I have done to satisfy myself. For the moment, I suggest that this is the best I can do.

*   *   *

If it is correct to say that the primary task of the fieldworker is to experience the rhythms, shadings, and emotional tones of social life, then it is also permissible to ask: What difference does such an analysis make? This question has no simple answer. But perhaps we can provide a rough outline of two major dimensions of any adequate response to the question: "Why fieldwork?"

First, fieldwork puts us directly in touch with the human dimensions of social life in a way that no other method of inquiry does. This is true because fieldwork forces us first to experience those dimensions and then to find words to describe them. Full understanding involves an intimate contact and this is what fieldwork provides. It allows us to describe a set of fundamental life experiences as they occur. Fieldwork supplies precisely what other methods of research drop out—the experiencing individual as a member of a community and the set of shared meanings that sustains that individual's action in an uncertain world. Fieldwork allows us to see social life as we live it.

But that is not all that fieldwork provides. It supplies us with an opportunity not just to describe the lives that we lead but to analyze them. When it is performed with skill, it allows us to examine the fit between principles and practice. Fieldwork, then, provides a mirror for looking at who we are as against who we would like to be. It provides us with soft data—observations, intuitions, and comments—for rethinking some very hard questions about what it means to be a member of the society.

NOTE

1. Charles Lidz, "Rethinking Rapport: Problems of Reciprocal Obligations in Participant Observation Research." Paper presented at the annual meeting of the Eastern Sociological Association, New York, March 1977. See also Marcel Mauss, *The Gift* (New York: W. W. Norton, 1967).

Epilogue

Vernon Boggs

Finding Your Spot

In a famous account of the process of getting into the field, Carlos Castaneda describes how Don Juan, the Yaqui Indian medicine man whom he sought as a mentor, refused to sponsor him until he had solved a riddle. He must find the spot (sitio) on the porch of the Indian's house where he could feel happy and strong. Not every place was good to sit or be on, the medicine man explained. Within the confines of the porch there was one spot that was unique, where the ethnographer could be at his very best. After a grueling night spent trying out first one and then another spot on the hard porch floor, Castaneda fell asleep in frustration. When he awoke, refreshed after a heavy sleep, the medicine man greeted him: "You have found the spot," he said.

Castaneda's metaphor describes the frustration and uncertainty all ethnographers experience as they seek to find the places and people with whom they will feel comfortable in developing their research. In this epilogue Vernon Boggs describes how he discovered that places that have had great meaning to him could become the "spots" for his research. He shows how he used the Afro-Hispanic dimension of his early experiences to formulate an ethnographic research project about black and latin cultural synthesis. As is true of many ethnographers, Boggs' motivations were at first highly subjective; he wished to gain a better understanding of some aspects of his own experience and upbringing. As a professional social scientist, however, Boggs also realized that his experiences afforded him certain insights into an important area of changing race and cultural relations.

Too often, he believes, jazz and blues have been interpreted as a unique cultural expression of the experience of Afro-Americans in North America. This view essentially ignores a powerful, ever-changing cultural idiom, rendering it a subject of history rather than a field for ethnographic exploration. Throughout much of Latin America, the Caribbean, and Africa, as well as in the cosmopolitan centers of the Western nations, jazz and local rhythms are being fused into new forms of popular music such as soucusse, pachanga, hi-life, and reggae. Boggs is part of a growing trend in the study of culture that traces the spread and synthesis of world cultures, in this case the Afro and Hispanic influences on New World music.

Boggs has written a number of articles on clave, the fundamental rhythm of Latin American musical traditions. At this writing he is deeply engaged in research on the origins of this cultural synthesis and the social institutions that sustain its growth.

When I was about 10 years old, my aunt asked me what I wanted for my upcoming birthday. I told her that I wanted a record called "Anabacoa." She promised to buy it if I could spell the name. I do not remember if I spelled it correctly or not, but I did get the record. Now, as I reflect on that early experience, I wonder how it was that such a record interested me so. I could not speak Spanish then. At home we heard only gospel music, and I have no idea why I was attracted to the latin sound. In any case, these early influences led me to wonder a great deal about my early experiences outside my own culture.

Another strong childhood memory is that of the cowboy movie. I began going to the movies alone at about 12 years of age. I particularly loved the Dracula-meets-Wolfman and Frankenstein flicks. Popeye was also a hero. But the cowboy films captured most of my attention. I identified with the Mexicans in those films. I began to dream of learning Spanish, and when I began high school, Spanish was my first elective course. I showed ability in language and was rewarded for my efforts, but I was also shy and doubted my linguistic abilities.

While in high school I hung out a great deal on the streets of Atlantic City, New Jersey, my hometown. This was during the 1950s, and "doo-wop," the early a capella form of rock and roll, reigned supreme. Sam Cook had recorded "My Baby Loves to Cha Cha Cha," and Ruth Brown had made a hit with "Mambo Baby." Again my attraction to the latin beat in black music took over, and while my friends and I stood outside the clubs on Kentucky Avenue, especially Club Harlem and Gracie's Little Belmont, I found myself impassioned by any jazz that included that latin beat. However, none of us had money to buy records, and the latin sound was especially hard to locate.

Then I heard the great Nat King Cole's recordings in Spanish, and I knew I had to have them. Here was a non-Hispanic singing beautiful melodies in Spanish. Somehow I managed to buy a copy. I played it over and over until I knew all the lyrics by heart. Then—still in the early 1950s—I heard about a club in New York City called the Palladium. I made up my mind to visit it and began saving my money from caddying at the local golf courses for a trip to New York.

One Friday evening in 1955 I took the bus to New York City. When I arrived, I took the subway to Harlem, a section of the city I knew nothing about. I found a cheap hotel room, and within a couple of hours I was at the Palladium Ballroom on 53rd and Broadway. Although technically I was too young to enter the club, I was allowed in. I still remember how the lighting and the music "blew me away." I felt that I was really and truly home. I had been looking for this music for years and this was it. I went back to New Jersey determined to spend as much time as I could at the Palladium.

In 1956 I joined the U.S. Naval Reserves, and in 1957 I was sent on active duty and assigned to the *U.S.S. Albemarle*. In 1958, as luck would have it, we were sent to Guantanamo, Cuba. I was in the heartland of clave, or Afro-Hispanic music, although I didn't know it at the time. From there we sailed to Montego Bay and Port of Spain, where I got a taste of reggae and calypso. Our next port of call was San Juan, Puerto Rico, the home of bomba and plena, two branches of clave.

I fell in love with San Juan. I went to a restaurant, found a jukebox, and played a record whose lyrics I did not fully understand and even today cause me some consternation. It was a song about a Negro who doesn't leave home because he's so ugly that whenever he does, the women who see him in the street faint. I probed the city for more Afro-Hispanic music. Curiously enough, I and some other servicemen found our way to a hot hangout in San Juan called the Palladium. What interested me about the place was that the same music was being played that I had heard in the States, except that it was not live. By the time my ship left San Juan, I had become a devotee of Afro-Hispanic music. I knew very little about its origins or rhythmic patterns—clave—but I loved it.

During the 1960s I began hanging out at the Palladium and Birdland in New York. My social life revolved around music: I went to dances at the St. George Hotel, Riverside Plaza, Hunt's Point Plaza, and other places too numerous to mention. I listened to Symphony Sid's nightly show and to Dick "Ricardo" Sugar. When Sid retired, I listened to his replacement, Joe Gaines. The Palladium folded in the mid-1960s, but aficionados of Afro-Hispanic music jammed the Cheetah on 52nd Street and 8th Avenue and the Village Gate, with its weekly Monday night series, "Salsa Meets Jazz," hosted by Symphony Sid. The music itself began to change from the mambo/cha cha craze to the latin boogaloo/charanga mode. However, in 1969 I began visiting Europe and within five years had moved there and become involved in research on other subjects. Music was on the back burner.

In the late 1970s I was a sociologist interested in urban ecology, deviance, and crime, but I did not realize that my love of Afro-Hispanic music could lead to professional research. But then I discovered that a colleague was teaching a course in the sociology of music. I suggested that he add a lecture on latin music, and he responded that his knowledge in this area was too limited and asked that I present the lecture. Although I accepted his offer, I realized that my knowledge of the subject was superficial in that everything I knew about the music had come from listening to it. If I was to address an audience on this subject, I would have to approach it more systematically.

I prepared my lecture on "Salsa Music" by reviewing my tapes of on-the-air discussions and conducting a review of the literature in various libraries and archives. I later edited the lecture and submitted it for publication in *Popular Music and Society*. Although these efforts were successful as far as they went, I realized that there was a great deal that was missing from my knowledge of the origins and spread of these musical forms. And so I began a more extensive research project.

Although the music I have been referring to is commonly called latin jazz, salsa, Afro-Cuban jazz, and other names, it is a genre that can most accurately be termed Afro-Hispanic because its roots are partly in Africa and partly in Europe and it is characteristic of Spanish-speaking societies in the Western Hemisphere. These facts were unknown to me for several decades. In addition to the racial component of the music, I also learned about its class component in the countries where it was "born." It had never occurred to me that before the 1970s this was considered lower-class black music in Afro-Hispanic societies. Even Cubans and Puerto Ricans classified it as such. Furthermore, I learned that Afro-Cuban musicians like Mario Bauza and Frank "Grillo" Machito had forged early alliances with Afro-American jazz musicians like Dizzy Gillespie and Charlie Parker in order to broaden the appeal of their music. And that while middle- and upper-class fair-skinned Cubans, Puerto Ricans, and other Hispanics shunned the music, middle- and upper-class fair-skinned American Jews and other American white ethnic groups supported and promoted it.

I had also noted in my travels that many white Europeans were fans of Afro-Hispanic music, just as they are collectors and fans of jazz. But this does not imply that clave is in danger of becoming only an art form (a problem faced by classical jazz in North America). Throughout much of latin America and Brazil, the Caribbean and Africa, and many large American cities, clave is a living cultural form with new dances and new variations emerging all the time. In fact, clave is a worldwide cultural complex.

A fortunate set of circumstances led me to realize that my lifelong love of music and language could also be a subject of professional research. Now I am deeply engaged in conducting interviews with the creators of Afro-Hispanic music. These valuable life histories are only part of my study, though. I have also found my spot in New York once again, this time among the radio personalities who keep the music alive in this city and help promote it throughout North America. From there my research will branch out to all locations where Afro-Hispanic music is performed and created anew. *¡Que viva la musica!*

Selected Bibliography

Anderson, Elijah. *A Place on the Corner*. Chicago: University of Chicago Press, 1978, 1988.

Bandolier, Adolph. *The Delight Makers*. Orlando, Fla.: Harcourt Brace Jovanovich, 1973/1891.

Becker, Howard. *The Outsiders: Studies in the Sociology of Deviance*. New York: Free Press, 1963.

Bernard, H. Russell. *Research Methods in Cultural Anthropology*. Newbury Park, Calif.: Sage Publications, 1988.

Boggs, Vernon W. "Salsa Music: The Latent Function of Slavery and Racialism." *Journal of Popular Music and Society* 11, no. 1 (Spring 1987): 7–14.

Boggs, Vernon W., and Rolf Meyersohn. "The Profile of a Bronx Salsero: Salsa's Still Alive!" *Journal of Popular Music and Society* 12, no. 4 (Winter 1988): 59–67.

Boggs, Vernon W., Sylvia Fava, and Gerald Handel, eds. *The Apple Sliced: Sociological Studies of New York City*. South Hadley, Mass.: Bergin & Garvey, 1984.

Bosk, Charles. "The Fieldworker as Watcher and Witness." *Hastings Center Report* 15, no. 3 (June 1985): 10–14.

Bosk, Charles L. *Forgive and Remember: Managing Medical Failure*. Chicago: University of Chicago Press, 1979.

Bradburn, Norman M., Seymour Sudman, and Associates. *Improving Interview Method and Questionnaire Design*. San Francisco: Jossey-Bass, 1981.

Castaneda, Carlos. *The Teachings of Don Juan: A Yaqui Way of Knowledge*. New York: Simon & Schuster, 1973.

Clifford, James, and George F. Marcus, eds. *Writing Culture: The Poetics and Politics of Ethnography.* Berkeley; University of California Press, 1986.

Epstein, Cynthia Fuchs. *Women in Law.* New York: Basic Books, 1981.

Erikson, Kai T. *Everything in Its Path: Destruction of Community in the Buffalo Creek Flood.* New York: Simon & Schuster, 1976.

Filstead, William J., ed. *Qualitative Methodology: Firsthand Involvement with the Social World.* Chicago: Markham, 1970.

Geertz, Clifford. *Interpretation of Cultures.* New York: Basic Books, 1973.

————. *Peddlers and Princes: Social Development and Economic Change in Two Indonesian Towns.* Chicago: University of Chicago Press, 1968.

Goffman, Erving. *Behavior in Public Places: Notes on the Social Organization of Gatherings.* New York: Free Press, 1966.

————. *Stigma: Notes on the Management of Spoiled Identity.* Englewood Cliffs, N.J.: Prentice-Hall, 1963.

————. *Presentation of Self in Everyday Life.* Garden City, N.Y.: Doubleday/ Anchor, 1959.

Griffin, John Howard. *Black Like Me.* Boston: Houghton Mifflin, 1960.

Halsell, Grace. *Soul Sister.* New York: World, 1969.

Hammond, Philip E., ed. *Sociologists at Work.* New York: Basic Books, 1964.

Harper, Douglas. *Working Knowledge: Skill and Community in a Small Shop.* Chicago: University of Chicago Press, 1987.

————. *Good Company.* Chicago: University of Chicago Press, 1982.

Horowitz, Ruth. "Remaining an Outsider: Membership as a Threat to Research Rapport." *Urban Life* 14, no. 4 (January 1986): 409–430.

————. *Honor and the American Dream: Culture and Identity in a Chicago Neighborhood.* New Brunswick, N.J.: Rutgers University Press, 1985.

Hughes, Everett. *The Sociological Eye: Selected Papers.* (New Brunswick, N.J.: Transaction, 1984).

Humphreys, Laud. *Tearoom Trade: Impersonal Sex in Public Places.* Hawthorne, N.Y.: Aldine de Gruyter, 1970, 1975.

Jacobs, Glenn, ed. *The Participant Observer: Encounters with Social Reality.* New York: George Braziller, 1970.

Kesey, Ken. *One Flew Over the Cuckoo's Nest.* New York: New American Library, 1962.

Kim, Illsoo. *New Urban Immigrants: The Korean Community in New York.* Princeton, N.J.: Princeton University Press, 1981.

Kornblum, William. "Working the Deuce." *Yale Review,* Spring 1988, pp. 355–367.

————. "Boyash Gypsies: Shantytown Ethnicity," in Farnham Rehfisch, ed. *Gypsies, Tinkers and Other Travellers.* New York: Academic Press, 1975.

————. *Blue Collar Community.* Chicago: University of Chicago Press, 1974.

Liebow, Elliot. *Tally's Corner: A Study of Negro Streetcorner Men.* Boston: Little, Brown, 1967.

Millman, Marcia. *The Unkindest Cut: Life in the Backrooms of Medicine.* New York: William Morrow, 1977.

Morales, Edmundo. *Cocaine: White Gold Rush in Peru.* Tucson: University of Arizona Press, 1989.

Myerhoff, Barbara. *Number Our Days.* New York: Simon & Schuster, 1978.

Nelson, William Javier. "Their Loss—Our Gain: The Gift of Latin Music to the U.S." *Afro-Hispanic Review* 6, no. 2 (May 1987): 19–24.

Schrank, Robert. *Ten Thousand Working Days*. Cambridge, Mass.: M.I.T. Press, 1978.

Stack, Carol. *All Our Kin*. New York: Harper & Row, 1974.

Wax, Rosalie. *Doing Fieldwork: Warnings and Advice*. Chicago: University of Chicago Press, 1971.

Whyte, William F. *Learning from the Field*. Newbury Park, Calif.: Sage Publications, 1984.

Whyte, William Foote. *Street Corner Society: The Social Structure of an Italian Slum*. Chicago: University of Chicago Press, 1943.

Williams, Terry. *The Cocaine Kids*. Reading, Mass.: Addison-Wesley, 1989.

Williams, Terry, and William Kornblum. *Growing Up Poor*. Lexington, Mass.: D. C. Heath/Lexington Books, 1985.

Wolfe, Tom. *The Electric Kool-Aid Acid Test*. New York: Bantam Books, 1983.

Zola, Irving Kenneth. *Missing Pieces: A Chronicle of Living with a Disability*. Philadelphia: Temple University Press, 1982.

Zuboff, Shoshanna. *In the Age of the Smart Machine: The Future of Work and Power*. New York: Basic Books, 1988.

Index

Contributors

ELIJAH ANDERSON, Professor of Sociology, University of Pennsylvania; Associate Director, Center for Urban Ethnography

VERNON BOGGS, Professor of Sociology, York College, City University of New York

CHARLES BOSK, Professor of Sociology, University of Pennsylvania

DOUGLAS HARPER, Professor of Sociology, State University of New York, Potsdam

RUTH HOROWITZ, Professor of Sociology, University of Delaware

LAUD HUMPHREYS (late), Professor of Sociology, Pitzer College

WILLIAM KORNBLUM, Professor of Sociology, City University of New York, Graduate School and University Center

ELLIOT LIEBOW, Visiting Professor, Catholic University of America (part time); Guest Researcher, National Institute of Mental Health

EDMUNDO MORALES, Project Director, Narcotics and Drug Research Inc., New York City.

BARBARA MYERHOFF (late), Professor of Anthropology, University of Southern California

CAROL STACK, Professor of Anthropology, Duke University

CLAIRE STERK, Research Associate, Center for Social Research, CUNY Graduate School; Visiting Scholar, Centers for Disease Control, Atlanta

WILLIAM F. WHYTE, Professor Emeritus, New York State School of Industrial and Labor Relations

TERRY WILLIAMS, Research Associate, Center for Social Research, CUNY Graduate School; Visiting Scholar, Russell Sage Foundation

About the Editors

CAROLYN D. SMITH is a writer and editorial consultant specializing in educational materials in the social sciences. WILLIAM KORNBLUM is the author of *Blue Collar Community* and *Growing Up Poor* (with Terry Williams). Kornblum and Smith have collaborated in the writing and development of textbooks on sociology and social problems.